ROLL DOWN YOUR WINDOW

ROLL DOWN YOUR WINDOW
Stories of a Forgotten America

JUAN GONZALEZ

VERSO

London • New York

First published by Verso 1995
© Juan Gonzalez 1995
All rights reserved

Verso
UK: 6 Meard Street, London W1V 3HR
USA: 180 Varick Street, New York NY 10014–4606

Verso is the imprint of New Left Books

ISBN 0–86091–449–6

British Library Cataloguing in Publication Data
A catalogue record for this book is available from the British Library

Library of Congress Cataloging-in-Publication Data
Gonzalez, Juan.
 Roll down your window: stories of a forgotten America / Juan
Gonzalez.
  p.   cm.
 ISBN 0–86091–449–6 (hbk).
 1. Hispanic Americans—Social conditions.   2. Hispanic Americans—
Economic conditions.   3. Poor—United States.   4. United States—Social
conditions—1980–   5. Puerto Rico—Economic conditions—1952–   6.
Haiti—Economic conditions—1971–   7. Central America—Economic
conditions—1979–   8. Mexico—Economic conditions—1982–   9. Latin
Americans—United States.   I. Title.
E184.S75G656   1995   95–20744
305.868—dc20   CIP

Typeset by M Rules
Printed and bound in Great Britain by
Biddles Ltd, Guildford and King's Lynn

CONTENTS

To my mother, Florinda,
and my daughters,
Melinda and Donishmaine,
for their love and understanding.

Special thanks
to New York's Daily News,
especially editors Gil Spencer, Jim Willse, Lou Colasuonno,
Martin Dunn and publisher Mort Zuckerman.
While we often differed in viewpoint, they have always
backed my reporting and my column as a necessary voice.

FOREWORD

THE PHONE WOKE me in my hotel room in San Antonio around 4 A.M. that April morning.

"Get up, get dressed and catch the first plane to LA," growled the caller at the other end. I immediately recognized the voice of my bulldog city editor, Hap Hairston, bristling with that whiplash excitement he always exudes when he's assumed command of a big breaking story.

"Are you crazy, Hap?" I grumbled, still half asleep. "I'm on vacation! What's the rush?"

"Where you been? Turn on the TV. The Rodney King jury acquitted those cops last night!"

"They did what?"

"Black folks are burning down the town. You can have all the vacation you want later, but right now I need you. And don't get yourself killed."

Hap used to joke that I'd been caught in so many riots, both as an East Harlem Young Lord in the 1960s and after that as a journalist perpetually drawn to run-down neighborhoods, that I'd become the paper's urban disorder "expert." Covering riots, Hap would say, a mischievous grin peeking between his bushy mustache and scraggly beard, is like skydiving or betting the mortgage on a single roulette spin – some get addicted to the rush of the risk.

By the time Los Angeles exploded in the spring of 1992, the editors at New York's *Daily News* had grudgingly come to accept me as a voice they needed. During its heyday in the 1950s, the *News* had been Superman's newspaper, boasting an unmatched circulation of 2.4 million, its own airplane, and the power to make presidents and movie stars alike quake before a front-page lashing. For generations it reigned as the most influential of brash big-city American tabloids, fashioning a special mix of lean, raucous writing and stridently conservative political content that became the staple of popular news delivery to this country's blue-collar working class. And in post-World War II New York that meant largely an Irish and Italian ethnic population. By the late 1980s, though, the city's population, as in most major urban areas, had changed face. Newly arrived African Americans from the South mixed with Hispanic and Asian immigrants to replace the older European settlers in unskilled jobs, and the newcomers soon proceeded to take over the inner-city ghettos, where chronic unemployment and welfare dependency dovetailed to create a permanent underclass riddled with crime and drugs. All of this prompted many of the *News*'s older readers to flee the decaying urban center for the mushrooming all-white suburbs that federal mortgages and highway construction funds had helped create. Belatedly, and somewhat reluctantly, *News* management realized that the paper must change or die, and as part of a new circulation strategy they suddenly decided to hire me away from the *Philadelphia Daily News*, where I'd been reporting for ten years, to write a regular column on New York, the city where I'd been raised.

When I started there in 1987, the *News* was still the largest urban daily in the country, though its circulation had plummeted to 1.3 million as television news established its mass appeal over print, throwing all city dailies into permanent circulation decline. The day I arrived was the last day of work for more than fifty veterans who had been forced into early retirement by a belt-tightening company buyout. From then on I was greeted each day by icy stares from many of the old-timers in the newsroom who would clench their jaws in silent disgust each time I passed. Quite a few naturally assumed I'd taken the seat of a more qualified white reporter just so the paper could meet some imaginary new minority quota. They regarded me as a menacing harbinger of the city's future. Not only was I a minority journalist (the first Puerto Rican to write a column at a New York newspaper in twenty years) on the staff of a traditionally Republican Irish-cop paper, but I was a left-wing radical one to boot!

Much of that changed in the winter of 1990–91. That was when the paper's parent, the giant Chicago-based Tribune Company, provoked a labor strike in an attempt to break the paper's craft unions, which over the years had won wages and benefits at the *News* that ranked us among the best-paid journalists in the publishing industry. A titanic five-month conflict ensued, one that became a rallying point for organized labor around the country, and I somehow emerged as the rank-and-file leader of the strike's 2,500 drivers, pressmen, mailers and reporters. Tribune Co. spent $400 million on the strike, only to lose most of its advertisers and watch helplessly as circulation dwindled to barely 400,000 copies a day. By the time the battle ended with our triumphant return to the newsroom and with Tribune's ignominious exit from New York publishing, the paper's old-timers, both in labor and management, had decided I was definitely qualified for *something*. At the final hour, Robert Maxwell, Great Britain's iconoclastic billionaire publisher, saved the paper by purchasing it from Tribune and negotiating a fair contract with the workforce. He even attended our victory party, held at the Park Avenue apartment of pro-labor socialite Lily Lawrence, and publicly toasted our unions. Not long afterward, however, Maxwell took a mysterious plunge into the Atlantic Ocean while sailing his yacht off the coast of Spain, in the process dragging his whole empire, including the *News*, down with him. Our savior, we learned within days of his death, had been a colossal scam artist and crook, and the paper was forced into bankruptcy. During the interminable bankruptcy proceedings many reporters opted for more secure jobs elsewhere, while a caretaker management reduced our travel expenses to rock bottom. In the midst of all this, the Los Angeles riot erupted. The editors could hardly afford to send a full complement of reporters and photographers for the saturation coverage the *News* would normally give an event of this magnitude. Thus, the origins of that call in the middle of the night to my hotel room in San Antonio.

After getting a sense of what kind of columns Hap wanted, I tossed on a T-shirt, jeans and sneakers, packed an overnight bag, and caught a 7 A.M. plane to Dallas, connecting there to a flight to Long Beach. (Los Angeles International had been closed at daybreak because there was too much smoke from raging fires.) At the small Long Beach terminal I called my newsroom in New York for wire service updates, purchased a street map, and dialed a couple of old friends in the area who might fill me in on South Central Los Angeles, the riot-torn neighborhood I was about to enter for the first time.

"Don't rent a blue or red car," warned David Sandoval, a Chicano who had grown up in the *barrio* of East Los Angeles. "Local gang colors. They'll make you a target. Another thing, there's plenty of *Raza* in South Central." Unknown to the outside world, Sandoval said, South Central had changed – once an all-black neighborhood, it had turned into a favorite settlement area for Central American immigrants, whose numbers now nearly equaled the blacks in population.

Over the years I've come to appreciate how knowing even the tiniest bit of information about a neighborhood – the kind of nugget you won't find in any Nexis search – can turn into a lifesaver when chaos strikes. Unfortunately, too many of us in American journalism parachute into disorders of this type like some John Wayne incarnation with a pen, usually well-protected either behind police lines or, in the case of network television stars, by a small army of private security guards. But to someone like me, Sandoval's tips were critical; they suggested there was at least a chance I could pass as a local. By 11 A.M. I was driving my rented car – a white Chevrolet – into the outskirts of the riot area, my window rolled down, my radio blaring local Salsa music, my notebook and street map stashed under the driver's seat. South Central, it didn't take me long to conclude, is not much different from East Harlem or Brooklyn's East New York section or the South Bronx or North Philadelphia, all of them notorious and violent neighborhoods where I'd lived for years at a time. And it does not approximate the squalor or random violence of some slums in Puerto Rico, like the old El Cano area of Santurce in the 1970s or San Juan's mammoth Lloren Torres public housing project today, or the many shanty towns of Latin America I'd come to know in Ciudad Juarez or Matamoros or Port-au-Prince or Santo Domingo. The better part of my life, in fact, has been spent living in or reporting from poor, outcast neighborhoods on our hemisphere's urban periphery, places most Americans never even see on Caribbean vacations and from which, should a wrong turn accidentally lead them there, they rapidly roll up their windows, tighten their grip on the steering wheel, and speed away.

By mid morning on the day of my arrival, the second day of the riot, the Los Angeles sky was already dark from hundreds of fires burning out of control. At some intersections every corner was ablaze, forcing me to speed past stoplights and through clouds of searing heat. A few times gangs of young black or Hispanic looters passed in front of my car, but they were so busy stealing they didn't stop to look at me. I parked and walked unnoticed into crowds still in the midst of wrecking whole shopping centers. Looters were so numerous their cars had to crawl bumper-to-bumper in and out of parking lots. Fire trucks and police cars, their sirens blaring, periodically sped by but rarely stopped to intervene. I talked to several looters as they carefully strapped freshly stolen mattresses to car roofs or gingerly hoisted new televisions and refrigerators into rusted pick-up trucks; to others who walked leisurely away with overflowing shopping carts or stumbled home, their backs bent under the weight of their pilfered loads. I talked, too, with frightened businessmen, armed and still desperately trying to defend their stores; with victims who had been burned out only hours before and now sat dazed and shocked in the rubble of their homes or shops; with others who were just trying to steer clear of the madness. Several times I had to jump back in the middle of an interview as fresh flames leapt wildly into the sky from yet another gutted building, showering embers and sudden bursts of swirling heat on the whole ghastly scene. For the next few days and nights I maneuvered with relative ease and in little direct danger through the middle of the worst civil disorder in America this century, and I did so simply by melting into the crowd. At night I would monitor the television reports that portrayed massive black anarchy, yet I had seen many Hispanics and even some whites involved in violence and looting that at times seemed almost methodical. I could not help feeling anger and despair at the images too many of my colleagues sent back: portraits that lacked texture or nuance, history or context. They were images that could only spark anger in Middle America, not comprehension. Being old enough to recall the fury and anguish that gripped this nation during the era of the great riots – Watts in 1965, Newark and Detroit in 1967, and the big explosions throughout the nation after King was killed in 1968 – I perceived Los Angeles as yet another tremor along the fault lines in our national being. South Central, after all, was no different in its essence from those neighborhoods where my own vision of reality, of right and wrong, had been shaped. In my early twenties I had tossed bottles and bricks at police during the East Harlem garbage riot of 1969 and the South Bronx gypsy cab driver protests of 1970, so the act of rioting has never seemed as irrational to me as it might to other journalists from more sheltered backgrounds.

Nor was the commonly accepted image of the cop on the beat as civilizer and protector part of my childhood experience. I had witnessed too many policemen in the neighborhoods where I grew up arbitrarily insult and abuse – even fatally shoot – random individuals, because the suspects in question were from a poor neighborhood, or had had a prior brush with the law, or spoke no English, or dared speak back. These cops did not feel that the standards of justice from the world outside the ghetto applied to us. So tell me, what is more alien to America, the journalist whose life experience permits him to understand the angry ghetto rioter, or the society which finds excuses for the lawless ghetto cop?

What deleterious images, after all, spring to mind nowadays from this moniker of alien. With McDonalds, Coca Cola and IBM scouring town marketplaces around the world for new outlets, hardly caring a whit what language the customer uses to buy their products, here at home the rest of us are busy fretting about the alien invasion or alien ideas ruining the nation. In a country where the citizenry's only claim to authentic Americanism is how early their parents got off the boat – or more recently, the plane or car – some of us have always been portrayed as alien no matter how long we have been a part of national life.

Certainly this is true for Native Americans. Even more so for blacks. In early 1995, as part of a regular panel of journalists on New York's public television station, WNET, I interviewed Peter Brimelow, a senior editor of *Forbes* who had just written *Alien Nation*, the latest in a spate of immigrant-bashing books. Brimelow, a recently naturalized British national, was fearfully concerned that he and his wife, a Canadian-born American, could not assure a comfortable future for their blond-haired, blue-eyed son unless the nation found the will to shut down further Third World immigration. What gall, I thought. Here was an Englishman telling me, a US citizen from birth, as were both my Puerto Rico-born parents and grandmother, about the alien problem.

This image of foreign or alien remnants within the body politic has even been turned against blue-collar Americans of all races whenever they have sought to organize associations or unions to improve their lot. Whether it was the immigrant labor scares that led to the Palmer raids of the 1920s, the McCarthyism of the 1950s, or the union scapegoating of the 1980s, much attention has been devoted by my colleagues in the press to proving how unnecessary unions are to American workers, and arguing how much better off they are confronting their bosses as individuals. At the same time, the day-to-day activities and conflicts at the workplace, perhaps the single most important set of experiences in the average person's life, are routinely ignored and underreported. The inside of a factory or construction site, thus, is as alien to most reporters as an urban black or Hispanic ghetto, or some poor white backwater community. So few journalists today have ever had to make a living through real manual labor that they fail to appreciate those millions of Americans who still perform factory work, fail to grasp how critical such labor still is to the modern lifestyle we take for granted.

More than a few of my columns are an attempt to view the world through the eyes of everyday working people. Maybe it was the decades my parents spent in sugar cane fields, factories and restaurants, or the six years after my Young Lords days when I labored in garment factories and printing plants, but I have been instinctively drawn to write about men and women who fight to maintain their basic working conditions or their livelihood. That my colleagues in the media could so easily ignore these periodic and often desperate stories in favor of more frivolous or entertaining news items has always seemed to me the most arrogant and nefarious exercise of our middle-class power.

When I returned to New York City in late 1987, after a fourteen-year absence, much had changed. The stock market crash two months earlier had sunk a generation of brash, high-living Wall Street yuppies and real estate speculators into the doldrums and tossed thousands on to the unemployment lines. The madness of unparalleled wealth side-by-side with massive homelessness was becoming indefensible. At the same time, the city was mesmerized and sharply divided by a series of racial conflicts, the most infamous of which, the Howard Beach case, involved a gang of white youths chasing and assaulting a group of blacks, murdering one. Meanwhile, the factories of Brooklyn, Queens and the South Bronx were fleeing to Asia, Central America and the Caribbean. Ed Koch was near the end of his reign as mayor, though few experts were prophesying his defeat.

The man who hired me at the *News* was Gil Spencer, who has since retired. Ask any writer who ever worked for him and the response will invariably be the same: few editors come any better than Spencer. "Hit hard and as often as you can," he told me my first day. Spencer genuinely believed controversy brought people closer to the truth. In a city brimming with extraordinary veteran newspaper columnists – Jimmy Breslin, Murray Kempton, Pete Hamill, Russell Baker, Sidney Schamberg – and awash with able younger writers, I figured my modest contribution would be a voice from another part of New York. Not writing *about* outcast neighborhoods, but *from* them. Not simply to entertain but to change. Not after the fact but before it, when coverage could still make a difference. In daily news-paper writing, as distinct from magazines or books, time becomes both an enemy and an ally. What you lose in the chance to chisel and refine for the relative few, you gain in the opportunity to influence and energize the many. I have tried to use as many columns as possible to probe the injustices visited upon the powerless. Yes, the rich and famous are also victims on occasion. But they have so many politicians, lobbyists, lawyers, gossip columnists, even editorial writers, ready to jump to their defense that they'll always do fine without my help. I prefer that desperate unknown reader who comes to me because he or she has gone everywhere else and no one will listen. More often than not I come across unexpected gems, human beings whose tragedies illuminate the landscape, whose courage hopefully inspires the reader to believe that there is indeed some greater good served by a free press than just chronicling or influencing the oustering of one group of politicians by another.

Not that I had always considered myself a dissident or radical journalist. During my teenage years at Franklin K. Lane High School in Brooklyn, I could safely have been called a conservative Catholic. As editor in chief of our school's newspaper, the *Lane Reporter*, I remember writing editorials condemning the militant black leader Reverend Milton Galamison for organizing student boycotts in New York schools to protest racism in the educational system.

I'm not sure I even considered myself a Puerto Rican back then, at least not until the first gang of Italians in East New York stopped me on the street near my house one night and threatened to beat me up for being one. Sure, I'd been born on the island, in a city called Ponce, and even returned there once with my parents to visit during a summer vacation. But I'd been raised from infancy in El Barrio, or Spanish Harlem, and then in East New York, and had spent all my educational years in American public schools. I had mastered English — not my native tongue — to such an extent that Lane awarded me top school honors in the subject at graduation. I considered myself a full American.

In 1965 a riot broke out in East Harlem over a white policeman beating a Puerto Rican. By then I was already a student at ivory-tower Columbia, immersed each night in the classics of Plato, Aristotle,

Aquinas, Rousseau, and the other apostles of European culture in Columbia's famous Contemporary Civilization curriculum. That I was being inculcated and socialized only with European heritage did not even dawn on me then. But out on the street, at the other end of a policeman's club, existed the more sober reality that no matter how well-educated we Puerto Ricans might become, Anglo society still considered us uncivilized, only slightly "better" than blacks, that we were living in the same poor neighborhoods as African Americans and being pummeled daily by the same official abuse and the invisible bullets of "benign neglect," as Senator Daniel Patrick Moynihan would later describe it.

By then the Vietnam War had begun to tear the nation apart. My Puerto Rican and black friends went off to war in crisply pressed uniforms and too many returned in drab pine caskets, always in higher percentages than their white comrades. At Columbia, where we Puerto Ricans numbered only a handful, we saw our affluent white Anglo classmates in open rebellion, not only against the war but against all that their parents had ordained for them – cookie-cutter dress and moral codes, cog wheel patriotism, the worship of technology, and the accumulation of artifacts. The heroes of the day were all rebels – Bob Dylan, Marvin Gaye, Abbie Hoffman, Stokely Carmichael, Rap Brown, Timothy Leary.

On April 4, 1968, Reverend Martin Luther King Jr, the country's moral compass, was assassinated in Memphis, Tennessee, where he had gone to support the black garbage workers' strike. Riots immediately erupted in more than 125 US cities and President Johnson called federal troops out to protect the capitol against Washington's black community. The nation seemed on the verge of civil war. A senior at Columbia when King was killed, I still remember vividly the overwhelming sense of upheaval and social chaos in the days following his death. Life as we knew it was hurtling out of control and the adults around us seemed both unable to explain it and powerless to stop it. With blacks and whites in open conflict, Puerto Ricans had no public figures to answer our questions about where our community fitted in.

Three weeks after King's death a student strike broke out against Columbia University's involvement with Vietnam War research and against the construction of a private university gymnasium on public land in nearby Morningside Park. Columbia, a smug and sprawling institution, is located right in the middle of Harlem. The gym, which was to be off limits to Harlem's black community, symbolized to many the university's long-time racist attitude toward its black neighbors. Several months earlier, I and several students had been arrested, in my first such brush with the law, during a civil disobedience protest in which we sat down in front of bulldozers at the gymnasium construction site at the urging of a young black minister.

Now, after King's death, white and black militant students, led by the Students for a Democratic Society (SDS) and the Student Afro-American Society (SAS), staged a series of sit-ins. In part because I was friendly with both SDS and SAS members, and perhaps because I was neither a white radical nor a black militant, I was chosen by the leaders of both sides to join the first coordinating committee for the protest. More than a thousand students were arrested and hundreds injured by police who occupied the campus on April 30 and there followed a five-week boycott of classes by more than 10,000 students. The strike and the violence at the historic Ivy League college polarized the city and reverberated across the nation, sparking scores of similar student sit-ins. Two months later, at the 1968 Olympic Games in Mexico City, when thousands of Mexican students protested against their own government, the Mexican army opened fire on the unarmed students and hundreds perished in a brutal massacre. Meanwhile, in France striking students sparked a nationwide general strike that toppled a government.

A generation had suddenly caught the fever of revolution. Those of us who were African American, Puerto Rican or Chicano began to awaken to the vast anticolonial movement that was simultaneously sweeping Asia, Africa and Latin America. We pounced on the books our college teachers had never deigned to show us – the works of Malcolm X and W.E.B. DuBois; Frantz Fanon and the Algerian revolution;

Kwame Nkrumah, Amilcar Cabral and Africa's anticolonial movement; Fidel Castro, Regis Debray, Che Guevara and the radical
educator of Latin America's poor, Pablo Freire. We began to regard
ourselves not merely as American citizens but as some newborn exten-
sion of the impoverished Third World within the United States.
Unlike the middle-class white students who rebelled alongside us, we
were mostly from poor or working-class backgrounds. The injustices
we marshaled against were not abstractions but problems imbedded in
the furrows of our parents' foreheads, daily reminders of what we had
endured as a people. At the time, however, none of us understood
clearly the why and the how of the Latino presence in the US. That
knowledge would come later.

A few weeks after the Columbia strike, a young Arab kitchen
worker, Sirhan Sirhan, assassinated Senator Robert Kennedy as he
campaigned for president in California, extinguishing with those fatal
bullets any hope of a quick end to the Vietnam War. A few months
later Tom Hayden, the soft-spoken SDS founder whom I had met during the Columbia strike, convinced me to go to Chicago to participate
in protests against the war that he, Yippie leader Abbie Hoffman,
peace activist David Dellinger, and Black Panther Chairman Bobby
Seale were organizing at the Democratic National Convention. For
several days I ran through the streets of the Chicago Loop with SDS
leaders Mike Klonsky, Mark Rudd, Bernadine Dohrn, Bill Ayers, Slim
Coleman, John Jacobs, Eric Mann, Susan Stern, Tom Hurwitz, and a
few thousand others, trying to disrupt the convention and somehow
force our nation to confront the holocaust that our B-52 carpet
bombings and Agent Orange chemical warfare were creating in
Vietnam. Chicago's rough and tumble mayor, Richard Daley, however,
was not about to allow anyone to spoil his moment of Democratic
party glory, so he ordered the police to move in. The violence that
ensued the night Hubert Humphrey was nominated the Democratic
party's standard bearer, with tear gas seeping into the convention hall
and overcoming delegates in full view of the network television cameras, only served to polarize the country further. Out of that tumult

and chaos, and the fear it engendered in Middle America of youth and black revolution, Richard Milhouse Nixon emerged a few months later as the nation's first law-and-order president. That fear, especially of the black power movement, became so strong that it catapulted Alabama governor George Wallace, then an unrepentant segregationist, into national political prominence as a third-party candidate. Wallace filled New York's Madison Square Garden with his supporters, and the Democratic party began splintering over the issue of race as working-class whites began their historic panic flight to the Republican party, a realignment of political forces that has never been reversed.

Even among liberals and radicals, the cleavage between the black and white races, whether in opposing Vietnam or fighting for civil rights, kept widening, and we in the fast-growing Latino community remained misunderstood and ignored by both. In the summer of 1969, I decided to leave the paternalism of the radical white movement to reconnect with my Puerto Rican roots in East Harlem. I joined with some college students to found the Sociedad de Albizu Campos, which we hoped would be a new Puerto Rican revolutionary group styled on both the old Nationalist party of Albizu Campos and the Oakland-based Black Panther party of Huey Newton and Eldridge Cleaver. After only a few weeks of meeting, we voted to merge with two other embryonic radical groups to form the Young Lords organization.

The original Young Lords were a Puerto Rican street gang from Chicago. At the time, gangs ruled ghetto life in that Midwest city much as they did in New York in the 1950s and do in Los Angeles today. The Mexican Latin Kings, the African American Blackstone Nation and the Puerto Rican Young Lords jealously guarded their neighborhood turf from one another and from the poor white hillbillies from the South. Jose "Cha Cha" Jimenez, the gang's natural leader, ended up in jail for a time, where he was befriended by a fiery black inmate named Fred Hampton, the legendary Black Panther party leader who would later be killed by Chicago police during an FBI-organized raid of the Panther offices. In jail, Hampton introduced Cha

Cha to the writings of Malcolm X, Guevara and China's Mao Ze Dong.

He talked about Puerto Ricans and blacks as oppressed people, about the need for the two communities to stop fighting each other. He used terms such as "serving the people" and "community control," and opened up a whole new world of ideas to young Cha Cha who, when he came out of jail in 1968, vowed to change his Young Lords into a Puerto Rican version of the Panthers. They adopted a purple beret and green army-surplus field jacket as a uniform and designed a button with a map of Puerto Rico and the slogan *Tengo Puerto Rico En Mi Corazon* (I Have Puerto Rico in my Heart) as an insignia.

By late 1968, the Chicago Young Lords were setting up breakfast programs for children, organizing local residents against Mayor Daley's urban renewal program in Chicago's Lincoln Park area, publishing their own newspaper and leading massive demonstrations against police brutality. They set up a headquarters in a church on Armitage Avenue and Dayton, which its liberal young minister later allowed them to use for a Young Lord breakfast program for hungry school children. Soon there were Young Lords chapters in Milwaukee, Waukegan and Los Angeles. A young Chicago-reared disciple of Martin Luther King Jr was beginning to organize a Poor People's March on Washington at the time – his name was Jesse Jackson. Long before Jackson ever devised the now-famous Rainbow Coalition concept, the Young Lords helped organize the first Rainbow – an alliance of the Black Panthers, Young Lords and Chicago's Young Patriots, a white hillbilly radical group.

In New York, those of us who started to organize La Sociedad de Albizu Campos read about the Young Lords in underground New Left publications, and a handful of us traveled to Chicago in a beat-up old Volkswagen in the summer of 1969 to secure Cha Cha's approval for starting the New York Young Lords. Among those early founders of the New York chapter were Felipe Luciano, already a well-known poet in the Harlem black nationalist scene; Pablo Yoruba Guzman, David Perez and Mickey Melendez, all of whom were attending an experimental program for minority students at the State University of New York at Old Westbury; Hiram Maristany, a brilliant photographer and lifelong resident of El Barrio; Sonia Ivany, a Cuban American who had recently left SDS; Carlos Rovira and Juan "Fi" Ortiz, two 15-year-old high school dropouts mature beyond their years; and myself, fresh from a year's involvement in the Columbia strike, the Chicago convention demonstrations and Students for a Democratic Society.

In the Lords, we began to study Puerto Rican history and advocate the view that Puerto Ricans were largely a black and mulatto people subject to discriminatory treatment not only because we were from a colony of the United States and spoke Spanish but because we were largely non-white. While this view of us as both a national and a racial group was fraught with erroneous assumptions – we are actually a multiracial people – it was an important step at the time to discovering our own identity, to affirming the black and mulatto aspect of our history that racism in Puerto Rico had attempted to deny. It also helped us understand that we had more in common with African Americans than with the rest of American society.

Within a year of our founding, the New York Young Lords emerged as the most explosive Puerto Rican political organization in mainland US history. Under the leadership of Felipe, Pablo, David Perez, Denise Oliver and myself, and assisted by other dedicated members such as Iris Morales, who went on to become an entertainment attorney, Richie Perez, now administrator of a huge vote participation project in New York, and Myrna Martinez, currently a New York Family Court Judge, we developed a reputation among the New York media as militants who skillfully mixed revolutionary messages with a stylish sense for modern public relations. It was no accident that many of us in the leadership later chose permanent careers in the media.

The essence of the new movement we sparked among a generation of Puerto Ricans was an affirmation of who we were – economic refugees from the last major colony of the United States who had seen it was necessary to defy the dominant Anglo society merely to survive.

We rejected its paternal insistence that we follow the path of our immigrant predecessors from Europe: the first generation accepting decades of second-class status while it established a foothold, the second being educated and assimilated quietly, and the third emerging as 100 percent melting-pot American.

But we were not just another immigrant group. Unlike the Italians or English or Poles, our homeland had been invaded and permanently occupied by Anglo-Americans, its wealth exploited to make fortunes for hundreds of US corporations, its patriots persecuted and jailed. Our experience, we decided in the Lords, was closer to that of the Algerians in France before independence or to the Catholics in Northern Ireland today. While for decades island school children had been taught from textbooks made in the US that we were incapable of self-government and that we would die of hunger without Uncle Sam, we concluded, just as the first books produced by a new generation of independent Puerto Rican scholars began to be published and confirmed our suspicions, that our tiny island homeland of Puerto Rico was as capable of being a prosperous independent nation as Israel or Taiwan or Jamaica or Switzerland.

I was twenty-six when I resigned from the Young Lords. By then most of the original founders had left, and the group had changed its name and degenerated into an obscure political sect. The reasons are so numerous that they are best addressed at another time and place. The essential ingredients of my view of the world, though, were already formed. A few years later I embarked on a new career in "mainstream" journalism that, as of this writing, is now seventeen years in the making.

Each set of journalistic eyes is conditioned and shaped by family upbringing, church and school training; is invariably limited by time, place, and the specific condition of the writer's social development; and is inevitably stamped with the unconscious imprint of his or her class, race, and gender. Each set of eyes necessarily becomes a flawed prism, partial or subjective by its very nature, through which the writer filters and then recreates an exceedingly complex reality. The battle to record history as it happens — from a divergent, sometimes unpopular view rather than from a consensus perspective already diluted by self-censorship — is the essential challenge to journalists in a modern capitalist democracy.

The men who run major media companies in America would have us believe that they are in the business of objectively informing the public. Most of us know better. Once, maybe, that was true. But today the giant chains and media conglomerates that run our daily newspapers, radio stations and television stations are principally in the business of making the maximum profit for restless shareholders, of getting the public to gobble up increasingly tinier and glossier bits of data that they label news or information and that they set adrift on their sea of advertisements. Some of the news is useful. Some is even accurate or at least entertaining. But most of it only serves either to confuse and divide or to divert the American people, making us less knowledgeable and less equipped to function as citizens. Even these old concepts of news are giving way before the giant corporate battles of the new information industry in this, the age when information itself has become the most critical of commodities. Each day the business sections of newspapers are filled with stories about the mergers and combinations of forces between telephone, cable, movie, entertainment, software, hardware and media companies. Whereas once aspiring young businessmen dreamed of running giant automotive, steel and rubber plants, today the mushrooming giants of corporate America are companies such as Microsoft, TimeWarner, TCI and Disney. The great war of the nineties is the one to determine who will have the most comprehensive access to your home through your television monitor, whether by fiber-optic phone lines, overground cable or satellite, to provide you interactively with all the data, news, entertainment and shopping services the captains of the megamedia hope to convince you to desire. The race is on to control your every waking hour, to charge for your every wish, to monitor your every opinion. At first glance, the democratization inherent in something like the new information superhighway, or the Internet, seems an undeniable boon to many, an obstacle to the control of the information flow by giant corporations. Yet the Internet functions only for that distinct minority of Americans who are already computer literate. So far it has only led to an ever-widening knowledge and information-access gap between that elite minority and the poor and working class of the country, especially most blacks and Hispanics. By the time the vast majority of Americans are connected to the information superhighway, I fear the megamedia companies will have already carved much of it up for their own ends.

Much of my time over the past two decades working in journalism has been spent rolling down windows for others in the outcast neighborhoods from which I came. The outsider who wanders into one of these neighborhoods by accident often registers only garbage and loud music, too many fatherless children being raised in chaos, government money being wasted. And with a roar of his engine, the stranger is gone. But had he rolled down his window and listened for a moment to the melancholy lyrics of the music, or stepped out and bought a cup of coffee at the friendly corner store, or talked to the housewife mopping down her front stoop, he might have learned something about his own humanity: the intricate spirit that evolves from learning as a child to ward off constant death; the unbending will to persevere; the sense of the real value of things that's fashioned from a life of working with your hands; the boundless ingenuity that comes from having so little yet needing so much; the sense of connection to a greater whole that comes from measuring your wealth not in objects acquired but in how many people love and depend on you. He might have realized that there are no pure people, neither in race nor in spirit, that black and brown, red, yellow and white are already enmeshed on this planet of ours in a common destiny, and that this is not a bad thing but rather the portent of a time when all human beings will be deemed family, worthy in and of themselves, their qualifications for a decent job judged solely by their real abilities, not on how they appear at first glance from the other side of a window.

I

NEW YORK, 1988–93

To the rest of the world, New York is seen as two sharply contrasting cities – the glamorous cultural capital of Broadway, Soho, Greenwich Village and the Upper East Side or the crime- and drug-ridden urban nightmare of the South Bronx and Bedford-Stuyvesant. Less known and far less chronicled are the few million New Yorkers who somehow manage to eke out a basic living despite the extremes of comfort and climate, despite constant job loss, run-down schools, diminished services and politicians who are masters at playing on their fears. This chapter examines New York after the stock market crash of October 1987 when all the glitter fell away to reveal a new Third World population existing side-by-side with the superwealthy. These were the last days of Ed Koch; the years of the city's first black mayor, David Dinkins; the heyday of Frank Lorenzo and Donald Trump; the era when the everyday rape of labor by corporate America became legal and acceptable, when racial hatred became ordinary fare.

THE THREE-FOOT snake did it.

"Drug dealers we got out of the building," Maria Figueroa explained. "Some nights I couldn't sleep keeping watch for them in the halls. But I wasn't fighting a snake. I prefer the drug dealers."

Neighbors say the reptile was left in front of Maria Guzman's apartment one day and roamed the building for three months, slithering into view first in one apartment, then slinking through a hole in a wall only to emerge from behind a refrigerator or out of a closet two floors below. The new tenant kept more people awake at night than the dealers.

"We called police. When they came they could never find it," said one resident of 1011 Carroll Place, a tiny street not far from Yankee Stadium. The hide-and-seek game between viper and residents continued until Guzman's husband and a neighbor cornered the slippery intruder and killed it. Everyone took photos of the corpse.

What does the snake have to do with a rent strike? Everything, say angry tenants. They believe it is the latest twist in the saga of their three-year dispute with Finkelstein-Morgan, the owners of 1011 Carroll Place, who, they charge, have used every trick in the book and then some. Finkelstein-Morgan own a lot of buildings in the Bronx, especially around the lower Grand Concourse. They've begun work on several co-op conversions in the area, and prices have been hurdling faster and higher than Edwin Moses on a good day. Add escalating building prices to a neighborhood where two years ago 60 percent of the tenants earned less than $10,000 a year and you have the highest housing dispossess rate in the city. Sure, you can tell yourself that those at risk are all lazy, unwilling to work or pay their bills. You may even believe it. Or you can admit that something must be done unless we want to see a doubling or tripling of the city's homeless population in the next two years.

What we have at 1011 Carroll Place is a rent strike, one which began in 1985 against the building's previous landlord for obvious reasons: the building had no heat, windows were rotten and useless, and the units had not been serviced for years. In response to the residents' protest, a judge at the housing court appointed a 7A administrator to run the building in the city's name. Almost immediately, Finkelstein-Morgan bought the property and promised repairs. As an act of faith, tenants settled with the firm and agreed in court to turn over a good portion of some $70,000 in withheld rent. For a year, Maria Figueroa collected rent on behalf of the tenants' association and delivered the monies to the new owners' Yonkers office, all the while insisting on the need for repairs. Some were made: new windows were installed, the roof was recoated, the elevator was serviced, and a few apartments were fixed. But many more were not. And when the owners started refusing to accept Section 8 vouchers from certain tenants, Figueroa became angry.

The association had set up a tenant patrol to keep out drug dealers. They claim a superintendent, appointed by the owners, removed the building's front lock to allow junkies easy access to the premises, and they also believe that several of the supers were addicts themselves. Frustrated and furious, the tenants restarted the strike and filed new complaints in the housing court. Immediately, a wave of dispossess notices arrived at 1011.

"I think it's sad. They're poor people. For so many years the building was run so poorly, they were able to get away paying eight months' rent a year instead of twelve. But that can't keep happening" is how owner Steven Finkelstein accounts for his company's heartless actions. Finkelstein says his firm has made almost all the necessary repairs, but that some tenants won't allow his repairmen to enter their apartments. The harassment allegations meet with denials. The snake, he insists, was not his agent.

The squabbling continues. Figueroa and the other tenants say that they're always willing to permit access, that the owners just use that excuse in court. Figueroa is also quick to point out that, since the back rent is in an escrow account, the tenants have not been trying to get away with anything.

I went to 1011 Carroll Place this week to tour the late snake's last home. In several apartments I saw gaping holes in the ceilings, rotten floorboards in the kitchens. In one tiny studio apartment, I met Maria Benitez and her three children. She pays $370 a month but has been notified that her rent will soon go up to $409, which is more than she can afford.

In the West Bronx, where most people don't make $10,000 a year, building prices are fueling a new gentrification wave, the poor are being pushed out again, and no one seems to care . . .

"THE WHITE SALE'S across the street in A&S, not in here. No talking allowed. Let's pretend we're in a courtroom."

"Carmen Rivera – final judgment, five days."

"Nick Siciliano – final judgment five days."

"Theresa Duncan – final judgment, five days."

"Patricia Martin – final judgment, five days.

The drone of the crowd grew louder as dozens of people wondered aloud about the decisions being handed out at breakneck speed. How on earth could a system work so efficiently and make so little sense?

"If we don't have absolute quiet, we'll just adjourn for two hours, people, and you'll all wait," scolded the clerk through his echoing microphone. "We've done it before."

He resumed reading off the list of landlords and tenants – those present, accounted for, and ready for the torture to follow. Welcome to calendar call at New York City Housing Court. The name should be changed to roll call because once you're on the list, you'd better turn up. If a landlord fails to appear, the case against the tenant is dismissed – not an ideal result. It is common for landlords – or their lawyers – to skip this bit of drudgework by hiring a stand-in. But the tenant who is not present to answer the first dispossess notice should beware! For him, a four-word sentence: "Final judgment, five days." If the tenant fails to make an appearance in five days, eviction follows.

This threat is not a foolproof deterrent. On my first visit to the Brooklyn housing court, thirty of the first seventy called were not present and consequently received five-day judgments. With their homes on the line, you'd think the parties involved would make an effort. What I've learned though, on this and subsequent trips, is that showing up has few rewards. This is how it goes: After a half-hour or so of waiting for your name in the calendar call, you're sent to a dungeonlike chamber and forced to vie with about eighty other disgruntled people for a dozen seats while you all wait to be assigned to a court-room upstairs. Once you're sent up there, don't expect to sit down. You'll have two choices: either to huddle in a suffocating, closet-sized courtroom or join the passing throng in hallways more akin to rush-hour train stations than to corridors of justice. If during this third waiting period the landlord doesn't succeed in forcing you to sign an agreement to pay all your back rent, the judge will then list your case for trial later that afternoon. You must now wait again, for the trial, which may or may not happen that day. Once in court, the chips are still stacked on the other side: 80 percent of tenants who appear before the judge do not have a lawyer; 80 percent of landlords do.

The stats tell the real story of calendar call. In 1987, there were 25,701 evictions in New York, an average of about a hundred every working day. [Serious business. After taking children away, throwing people out of their homes is the most violent act the state can commit against its citizens.] . . .

THEY SURPRISED Artie Biagi, the captain of the tugboat *Miriam Moran*, early on the morning of February 15, 1988, at the Staten Island pier. A company supervisor and a couple of security guards barged into the cabin, woke Biagi, and threw him off his boat. To secure it, they said. To be fair, it wasn't really Biagi's craft. The title belonged to Moran Towing and Transportation Company. All the same, if you've worked for a company for forty-two years and have been captain of the same boat for decades, you can be excused for thinking proprietarily.

The strike started the following day and ninety-seven days later it's still on. Last week, it became the longest tugboat strike in New

York's history, and no one in this city, except the members of Local 333, has even noticed. This is winter in America for organized labor. It's an unrelenting cold spell that started back in August 1981 when Ronald Reagan threw 11,400 striking air traffic controllers into the street after firing the lot of them for refusing to comply with his return-to-work order. Since then, we've had nearly a decade of give-backs, takebacks, cutbacks and every other kind of backlash to American labor. Unions have been left with two choices: concede or be crushed.

Al Cornette is president of Local 333. He's had 2,500 men on the picket line for ninety-seven days. He and his men didn't want the strike, but couldn't see a way out of it. What can you do when management demands a 30 percent or more pay reduction; proposes to eliminate vacations, overtime pay and holidays; and wants to reduce the number of workers on boats and barges? What can you do when they refuse binding arbitration?

On the management side, there is divided opinion about the strike. Some twenty-five of the smaller companies that operate tugboats, barges, and tankers in the port agreed to contracts with the union. Most of these, however, provide no pay raise for workers and no cost-of-living increase until the third year. The nine biggest operators chose a showdown.

The last major port strike was in 1979 and ran for eighty-eight days. When city trash collection slowed because barges couldn't take trash to landfills and heating-oil shortages developed as tankers were diverted to other ports, the union finally won a big contract and the dispute was settled. But a lot has changed since then. The city's trash is disposed of under a separate contract and the companies have imported hundreds of unemployed ship hands from the South to keep 120 tugs and 120 petroleum barges afloat.

This time, the proud, rebellious longshoremen's union, a throwback to labor's heyday, is going to be humbled. "I don't think the companies are in any mood to settle this thing" was the opinion of one industry official. The companies themselves have refused to comment on the dispute, although they have complained in the past that labor costs in New York are too high. Cornette boasts that his members are "the highest paid boatworkers in the world," earning on average $31,000 a year, but he is quick to point out that the companies are not exactly losing money: the union is willing to agree to some concessions, but not to be raped.

His members are behind him. There have been violent moments in this strike – scuffles on picket lines, shots fired at scabs, a firebomb attempt on a tugboat. Understandable behavior. Take a man's paycheck away, set him back twenty years economically, march out-of-town replacement workers past his picket line every day, then sermonize about violence and watch your words fall on deaf ears.

This is a strike the longshoremen didn't want and one they can't win. Somehow, though, when you battle rivers, winds and the ocean for a living, pompous bottom-liners don't bend your knees too much. As one tugboat captain, a Vietnam veteran, told me: "It's easy to exploit freedom when you haven't had to fight for it." What hurts these men most, though, are the other unions. A few have shown support, but most have looked the other way, as if their future wasn't in some way linked to Local 333's.

The rest of New York hasn't even blinked. "It's the greatest non-event in the city," said Robert Greenes, spokesman for the New York Oil Heating Association, of the record-long strike. When winter in America began for labor in 1981 with the air traffic controllers, the public paid more attention. Seven frigid years later, union busting doesn't even make news . . .

Postscript: Two years later, I met Dan Kremer in a bar on Ocean Avenue in Valley Stream, Long Island. Dan bought the bar for his wife in 1985 and fixed it up on weekends. The place brings in just enough money to pay the rent and keep food on the family's table. Dan hasn't had a regular-paying job in two years. That's how long this 55-year-old tugboat worker has been on strike, give or take a few weeks.

What's happened in the two years since the "greatest non-event" in city history began? Well, while the membership of Local 333 has been out on the line, the number of oil spills in New York harbor has increased steadily – from 342 in 1988, to 368 in 1989, to a whopping 120 in just the first two months of 1990 – according to Coast Guard statistics. Every time Dan Kremer hears about a new oil spill in local waterways, he just shakes his head.

It's simple, says Al Cornette. "Too many inexperienced and incompetent non-union crews are running ships in and out of the harbor." The region's nine major tug and barge transport companies have been using hundreds of strikebreakers imported from the South to pilot and operate boats. Nobody calls them scabs anymore. Since Reagan, there's a new name: replacement workers. That's the sort of title you'd give a rebuilt master cylinder or alternator for your car. In this case, however, these replacements are replacing workers whose families have been thrown into economic chaos. And, in this case, they're wreaking havoc on the environment as well . . .

LADY BING AND her husband, former Metropolitan Opera impresario Sir Rudolf Bing, were once the talk of the town. Last week, Lady Bing could be found on a stoop outside the Ginger Man restaurant on the West Side, homeless and destitute. How to explain this perverse, reverse fairytale?

Carroll Douglass shocked New York society a few years ago when she eloped to Virginia and married Sir Rudolf. He was eighty-five and suffering from Alzheimer's disease; she was forty-seven with a history of mental problems. Four years before the marriage, a court had given Carroll's brother and sister power over her finances after she developed a fixation for the Pope and tried to buy a $40,000 helicopter to become the Holy Father's pilot. Two days after the wedding, another judge decided that Sir Rudolf was incapable of managing his own affairs and put his long-time friend and lawyer Paul Guth in charge of his welfare.

There followed a series of long legal battles waged by Sir Rudolf's lawyers to annul his marriage to this "deranged gold digger." (A questionable bit of labeling by Guth: while it is true that Carroll Douglass had a history of being attracted to older men and had married twice before, it is also the case that she was a well-to-do Washingtonian with a sizeable inheritance of her own.) In the meantime, Lady Bing kept disappearing, escaping to Florida, Britain and Anguilla with her new hubby despite judges' orders to stay close to their Essex House apartment. When she did return home, she had to be ordered away from Sir Rudolf for a few hours each day so that a nurse could care for him. Guards were hired to prevent her from whisking him away again.

In the claustrophobic world of New York high society, the Bings were a scandalous item, a wholly original pair prone to public outbursts of the most inappropriate kind. It was charged in court that the couple engaged in "inappropriate sexual behavior" in the lobby of their apartment building and even at the opera. The man who once ruled the Met with an iron baton was turned away from his own box at the opera house, and he and his wife were often spotted in the standing-only section. Naturally, there were big scenes in restaurants. All in all, it wasn't exactly a marriage made in heaven.

Today, this friskiness knows no home. Last May, Sir Rudolf was placed in Riverdale's Hebrew Home for the Aged. His fortune, once valued at $900,000, had dwindled to $30,000. Forced to leave Essex House, Lady Bing wound up on the streets last week. Staff members from a Goddard-Riverside Community Center outreach project found her on Wednesday and took her to the West Side Y, where single rooms without bath run to $32 a night.

I went to visit her. She had been given a room at the end of a dingy L-shaped corridor, near a fire exit. I knocked several times. No answer. As I pushed a note under her door, I thought back to newspaper photos of Sir Rudolf and Lady Bing on their luxurious lovebird vacation only two years ago. Unbeknownst to me, Lady Bing had been moved from the Y to Bellevue's psychiatric ward, the latest of several mental wards she's been in over the years. When I learned of this relocation, I tried unsuccessfully to reach her brother in Washington and her aunt and uncle in Arizona, to see if anyone knew that Lady Bing was homeless and in Bellevue. No one returned my calls, not even her lawyer, Harvey Sladkus. Finally, I placed a call to Bellevue, to the pay phone on her ward, and asked for Carroll Douglass Bing.

"Carroll? Hold on, I'll get her," said the woman who answered.

After a few minutes, a silk-soft voice whispered, "Yes, this is Carroll Bing."

I identified myself as a reporter and mentioned the note I'd left at the Y.

"Oh, yes. Can you hold on just one minute, please?" was the reply.

A short while later, another woman came to the phone.

"Who you waiting to talk to?"

"Carroll Douglass Bing. She was just talking to me."

"Yeah, well, she just walked away. She looks a little confused, a little lost. I don't think she can talk right now. Call back later."

I called Rudolf Bing at the Hebrew Home for the Aged.

"Sir Rudolf can't talk now. He's indisposed," said a man with a British accent who referred to himself as Bing's nurse.

When was the last time Sir Rudolf saw his wife? I asked.

"It was some time ago. I'm afraid I can't answer any questions. I hope you understand," he apologized.

Now Sir Rudolf, his mind practically shot, sits alone in an old folks' home with his nurse, while his wife is homeless in Bellevue's psychiatric ward. Once again, reason and law have prevailed over love and passion.

SANDY-HAIRED Sylvia Cain kept ringing her bell on the sidewalk in front of Grand Central Terminal on the coldest December 12 New Yorkers could ever recall. She had been standing, blue-capped and bright-eyed, in the numbing chill for hours and it was only noon. Beside her a megaphone blared Christmas carols into the frosty air. Few human beings stand still in near-zero weather for hours on end – unless, of course, they are members of the Salvation Army collecting money for the needy and Christmas is coming. Sylvia Cain is one such soldier.

Some blocks away, 67-year-old Ann Pankowski, one of the needy, was worried because that very Army was forcing her from her home of twenty-two years – as long a time as young Sylvia has walked this earth – and on to those freezing, carol-filled streets.

Nothing that follows is meant to suggest that the Salvation Army, the legacy of a nineteenth-century English evangelical Christian named William Booth, is anything but committed to the "love of God and a practical concern for the needs of humanity," as its literature professes. It's just that I don't like to see elderly ladies forced out of their homes, no matter who does it and for what reason.

This Christmas carol begins at the Anthony Residence on East 29th Street, a building the Army has owned and operated for decades which rents 170 single rooms to working women. According to a spokesman for the organization, the residence was meant to "provide a Christian environment to keep fine girls from the country away from the evils of the city." For years, however, the Anthony rented rooms not only to young single working women but also to older women who were mentally or physically disabled. The building was even licensed by the State Department of Social Services as an adult-care facility. (The state pays $660 per month per woman, which includes three meals a day. The younger tenants pay $550 a month for a room and two meals daily.)

This is how Ann Pankowski arrived on October 10, 1966. "I was married and living in Middletown before my nervous breakdown," she recalled. "From the state hospital they sent me here. I like it. It's near the subway and buses and all the big stores. We have security at night." Her companions at the Anthony agree. Winifred Waite, a 64-year-old Englishwoman, arrived twelve years ago after knee replacement surgery. Told she would never walk again, Winifred now hobbles efficiently through the Murray Hill neighborhood with the aid of a cane. Irene O'Neill, aged sixty-two, arrived six years ago after her husband died. "I made friends with the other ladies. A lot of us figured we'd last here for whatever years are left, relax and enjoy life."

About a year ago, conditions at the residence began to change after Major Gerald Spencer and his wife took over the running of the place and the Army had the building decertified for adult care. Once, the building had housed more than a hundred women under the state program; in 1987, at the time of decertification, only sixty were left. Army and state officials informed these remaining tenants that they would be moved to other homes, mostly in the suburbs or outer boroughs of the city. Some have now left. Relocation, though, is neither straightforward nor desirable for the seniors. Winifred's concerns echo many of her fellow residents': "I don't want to go to one of these places far away from my doctor, with two in a room and one closet." It's an ugly, mean situation. As Ann reports, "Some of the tenants are very timid. We're being harassed to leave."

I called Major Spencer to discuss these developments. He refused to comment and referred me to the Army's lawyer, who would speak but asked not to be identified. According to him, as the number of state-funded tenants in the building declined, the extra nursing care required by law became too expensive to maintain. "The Salvation Army is hard-pressed to come up with the money and they can't do everything," the lawyer said. Of the women whose homes may be lost, he was kind but firm: "We're not interested in forcing them out and they're not going to get kicked out in the street. We're giving thirty-day notices in January to the handful who do not want to move. They'll realize the Salvation Army is serious."

Sylvia Cain, originally from Akron, Ohio, is a cadet now. All first-year cadets have done what she was doing yesterday, ringing bells on street corners and collecting money at Christmas, ever since William Booth founded the Army in 1865. A wondrous smile came over her face as she described two panhandlers, one shoeless, who had deposited their entire daily take into her bucket. Some might call that God's work, others insanity . . .

*

JOSE BORJA came to this country from Ecuador forty-four years ago, arriving in New York at age sixteen after working his way around the world on a Panamanian freighter. He joined the Merchant Marine and served in World War II on the cargo ship *Payne Wingate*, helping transport American soldiers and weapons through the Nazi blockades to Europe. Later, Borja became a US citizen and two of his sons joined the armed forces. His eldest, George, was wounded in eleven spots by grenade fragments in Vietnam and never fully recovered. A few shards lodged in his brain and made for a lifetime of throbbing headaches, pure agony. Last April, George died in the veterans' hospital in the Bronx. He was thirty-nine years old. Borja's younger son served in the Navy for seven years, mostly aboard aircraft carriers in the Middle East.

For thirteen years, while he persevered toward his dream of becoming a successful novelist, Borja worked as a waiter at the exclusive Grand Tier Restaurant of the Metropolitan Opera in Lincoln Center. "I remember having conversations with [UN Secretary-General Javier] Perez de Cuellar and serving General MacArthur's widow every Saturday, as well as Imelda Marcos," Borja says proudly. Two years ago, he and his coworkers were thrown into the street by the company that was operating the restaurant for the Met.

Thus, the subject of our story: whether Latinos and blacks, who are good enough to die fighting for this country and to wash dishes and clean tables at New York's finest restaurants, are equipped to be waiters and bartenders to the affluent. It asks whether or not, on the island of Manhattan, mixing a screwdriver and serving scallops has somehow become an inherited skill of young whites when good tips and a decent living are at stake.

You see, before 1986 most of the nearly one hundred workers at the Grand Tier were Hispanic. Many were in their fifties and, like Borja's friend, Mario Marin, had worked there for over twenty years. Two years ago, Met officials decided to change the restaurant's management company to an outside outfit called Restaurant Associates.

Their rationale had the familiar ring of current union-busting corporate speak. As David Reuben, public relations person for the Met, explains: "We just felt it was time for a change." There had been complaints about "the quality of service," according to Restaurant Associates' lawyer Richard Schaeffer. The Met, he claims, wanted "a staff that would have greater excellence."

This would come to mean paler and younger. When the opera season opened in September, almost all the old employees were fired, replaced by a new crew of fresh-faced, white bartenders and waiters. The old staff complained to their representatives, Local 100 of the Hotel and Restaurant Employees Union, to little avail. They say union leader Anthony (Chickie) Amodeo, whom federal prosecutors have accused in court of controlling the union for the Gambino crime family, was singularly unhelpful, despite the fact that a year was left on their union contract.

Of course, the Met's actions were hardly unique. During that same year, the United Nations Restaurant pulled a similar staff change with Restaurant Associates in charge, and the famed "21" club closed and then reopened, having replaced about fifty older workers, many Hispanic, with younger ones. In the latter case, ex-workers picketed the club despite the opposition of their union – Local 100, again – and filed a discrimination suit. Last week, fired "21" club workers quietly won an estimated $1.2 million settlement.

Recently, I've had a chance to enter a few of these obscenely expensive midtown restaurants, and many more of the ordinarily overpriced variety. The kitchen workforces are invariably teeming with underpaid Hispanics; the waiters and bar staff are almost uniformly white. Top officials at the Met probably know nothing about this and may not even have noticed the change. They care little about what Jose Borja and his family have done to serve their adopted country. They wouldn't descend from their operatic fog to worry about a 61-year-old man who can't find a job – that is, not since he was fired from the restaurant they own . . .

*

AFTER VIEWING Felix Resto's body at the Ortiz Funeral Home in the Bronx, I headed straight for the phone booth at 106th Street and Madison Avenue in East Harlem. It was close to five o'clock on a dark February day and a piercing wind had begun to whip the streets when I arrived at the corner. There was no one standing around. Still, I waited for several minutes, hoping some young thug would pass by and try to claim the public phone as his office line, hoping I might meet the gaze of some person Felix had spent all of his time trying to help – and who, in the end, returned the kindness with a beating and a bullet in the back.

Felix was thirty-five years old when he died last Thursday night in his wife Linda's arms on that very corner. I met him some twenty years ago when, as a teenager, he joined the Young Lords party and worked in our office on Longwood Avenue and Kelly Street in the Bronx. Like most of us then, he was a rebellious spirit, determined to get respect for Puerto Ricans.

When the Young Lords disbanded in the mid seventies, I moved to Philadelphia and Felix, like so many others, floundered for a while. For a few years, friends say, the heroin habit got to him, but he soon overcame it. Once he met Linda, she became his anchor. They married and had three children. Felix worked at a series of jobs to keep the family afloat. Most recently, he had been a city employee working with the Human Rights Commission. At a Neighborhood Stabilization Office in Queens, Felix led education programs for immigrant workers and taught local tenants how to organize effectively. "Everyone in our neighborhood knew and loved him," said Ivette Bernabe, president of the 40th Street Block Association in Woodside. "He helped our building get a rent reduction for each apartment by teaching us about housing law." His dream was to go to law school; this year he finally applied, with the hope of starting in September.

Then came Thursday night. Because of financial difficulties, Felix and Linda had fallen behind on their phone bill and their service had been cut off. Around 8 P.M., Felix left their apartment to go to the corner phone booth to call a coworker about a case. When he reached the booth, police say, three young men refused to let him use the phone – they needed it for business. Never one to be intimidated, Felix argued with them and the trio attacked.

"He came running upstairs and yelled to one of the kids to get his baseball bat," Linda recalls. "He told me some guys had jumped him outside and he was going back to find them." When Felix ran out of the apartment, Linda threw a coat over her nightgown and rushed after him. "By the time I got down to the street," she said, "he was already on the ground. They had shot him in the back – it's just not fair."

Yesterday, I stared at the booth where Felix met his killers and tried to imagine what I would have done in his place, what any of us can be expected to do in the age of crack when young thugs tell you that you can't use the public phone on your own corner. And then I thought of all the politicians, including Governor Cuomo, who talk so much trash about fighting drugs while they play shell games with state and city budgets before throwing chump change at the drug problem. And I kept seeing Felix Resto in his casket, having lived and lost his life for the same thing: A little respect . . .

Eastern Airlines picket line, week one:
Garry Hagstrom has been an Eastern Airlines mechanic for twenty-one years, yet this is week one of his first strike. "That's a good record for our union," Hagstrom said, ears glued to a walkie-talkie and eyes fixed on the runway below, as he monitored, from a second-floor terminal window, the few Eastern planes that departed yesterday from LaGuardia Airport. Outside, two dozen of his union brothers picketed in the ice and snow.

Since there's been so much commotion since the strike began on March 4, 1989, about the inconvenience to stranded airline travelers – and the threats of inconvenience to railroad commuters – it's high time someone talked about the rape of one of this nation's major companies and about the decimation of the livelihoods of thousands of loyal employees by a corporate Genghis Khan named Frank Lorenzo. Who is Frank Lorenzo? The man at the helm of the largest airline operation in the non-Communist world – Texas Air – and probably this country's biggest union buster.

When Lorenzo took over Continental in 1983, he declared bankruptcy, broke all union contracts and laid off thousands to cut costs. The results have hardly been impressive: Continental continues to hemorrhage money and has been plagued with traveler complaints ever since. But this is of little concern to Lorenzo or Texas Air, an organization in which the subsidiaries lose obscene amounts of money while the parent company grows ever richer. Through Texas Air, Lorenzo has gained control not only of Continental and Eastern, but of the now-defunct People Express, Frontier and New York Air as well. According to the *Wall Street Journal*, the individual companies have lost a half-billion dollars each in 1987–88, but through a series of management fees, rents and commissions, Texas Air raked in $150 million in 1987 alone. Lorenzo performs these financial hijinks by arranging sweet deals between his many holdings. For instance, he sold Eastern's computerized reservation system to Texas Air for $100 million although it was estimated to be worth more than $200 million. Most of the purchase price was financed by Eastern at 6.5 percent interest. (You can get more for your money in the bank.) As soon as the deal was done, Lorenzo turned around and had Eastern pay Texas Air $130 million annually for the same service.

Lorenzo vigorously denies that he is trying to liquidate Eastern, but the employees on the line read his actions differently. "He wants to change the whole marketplace to pay everybody five dollars an hour. You can't get professional service for that kind of pay," said William Clark, one of the picketers from the International Association of Machinists. Clark has put in eleven years at Eastern, parking planes as they arrive, loading and unloading in bitter cold and sweltering heat, nights and weekends, and he's still not earning the top wage of $15 an hour. Clark takes home $340 a week, with which he supports a wife, two kids and a mortgage on Long Island. Frank Lorenzo wants to cut his pay in half.

The machinists have tried to be reasonable. Their contract expired fifteen months ago, yet they kept negotiating. They offered to go to binding arbitration. Lorenzo refused. They urged President Bush to name a federal panel for a sixty-day cooling-off period. Bush refused. There is every indication that Bush is looking to repeat Ronald Reagan's stand on the air controllers' strike and teach organized labor another lesson.

This time, it will come at a price. The pilots have refused to cross the machinists' lines, as have the flight attendants. Without pilots, planes don't fly. Never has an American airline been so paralyzed in the face of labor unity as has Eastern these last few days. "The company may go down with this strike," one pilot reasoned, "but he [Lorenzo] was taking it down anyway. We had no choice." Over at TWA, mechanics whose contract talks are at an impasse are eager to join their brothers at Eastern.

Organized labor, its face puffy from a decade of lumps in the anti-labor Reagan era, now finds itself in the biggest brawl of its modern life, toe-to-toe against a corporate Genghis Khan . . .

Eastern Airlines picket line, day ten:
When you're on strike, ten days can seem more like ten months. All the old routines, the markers that guide and anchor life on the job, are suddenly gone. Overnight, strangers become close pals; friends change into enemies. The press, the courts, the government, the public, even union leaders, reveal sides of themselves you never saw before – while each day you walk the line and worry about your family's future.

On day ten of the Eastern Airlines strike, you could read anger in the face of Henry Krawczyk. Krawczyk has been a mechanic for Eastern for seventeen years, ever since he came to the US from Poland, a country whose strikes hold more interest for the folks in Washington than do our own. These days, his rage is targeted at one man – Frank Lorenzo – to whose company he's given nearly two decades of his working life. "We took an eighteen percent cut a few years ago," Krawczyk recalled bitterly. "What happened to all that money they saved then?" But the Eastern mechanics walking the line at LaGuardia have given more than just money to Lorenzo's company. I was reminded of their working conditions by one of Krawczyk's fellow strikers: "Do you know what it's like doing maintenance in twenty-five- and thirty-degree weather at night, on top of an icy metal wing with the wind whipping in your face? You can't wear gloves 'cause they're too bulky to handle bolts or parts, so your hands just turn numb." At LaGuardia, there are no hangars for the Eastern planes.

Outside, on the picket line, tempers boil over in the freezing cold. Inside, it's a different story. At the Eastern Shuttle terminal, business is brisk, with college students and bargain-hunters taking advantage of the half-price, $49 singles to Boston and Washington that the company is offering to win back passengers. The strike, though, has become a war of attrition. Despite having more than $400 million in cash reserves, Lorenzo declared bankruptcy last week, defaulted on millions of dollars' worth of tickets, and refused to pay the strikers their last week's wages.

Lorenzo had counted on the lack of unity and the class differences between pilots, mechanics and flight attendants to impose his will and his salary structure on Eastern employees. But his pilots surprised him. They believe their company can be as well-run and profitable as Delta, American or United and still have a management that respects the workers. As one pilot told me, "Employees with good morale produce better. We won't work for Frank Lorenzo." Their support for the mechanics may make or break the strike. Eastern has announced plans to expand air service to a few more cities, but to do so the airline needs pilots. According to federal regulations, a pilot can only fly thirty hours in seven days, one hundred hours a month. Thus, the company can't work its few strike-breaking pilots overtime, nor can it quickly bring in pilots who aren't Eastern-trained. By the end of this month, who will fly the planes?

Meanwhile, Federal Judge Robert Patterson keeps extending a restraining order to prevent the rail unions from joining in a sympathy strike – an action which would be legal, union leaders claim, given the terms of the Federal Railway Act. President Bush has so far refused to intervene in the dispute unless there is a sympathy strike, in which case he'll move quickly to crush it. He might have to. Three busloads of bus drivers from Transport Workers Union Local 100 joined the striking Eastern workers on the picket line yesterday and organized support is growing. The international president of the 100,000-member union, George Leitz, threatened a "nationwide transportation walkout" to force government action on the strike if the court injunction is lifted.

Therefore, after just ten days, the Eastern Airlines strike of 1989 is rapidly becoming the most important labor–management fight of our generation. You know, the experts keep talking about how weak organized labor has become, always quick to point out that not even two out of every ten American workers are in a union. Those experts, though, seem to forget that that small percentage is concentrated in the lifeblood industries of this nation: transportation, auto, steel and government itself. Those experts don't understand that you can only keep taking – money, time, dignity – from people for so long because, sooner or later, those people will fight back, no matter the threats or the dangers. Today, on day ten, Frank Lorenzo and the nation have begun to find out just how strong labor really is. Strikes have a way of doing that . . .

Eastern Airlines picket line, ten weeks later:
Ursula Van Der Horst instantly recognized the woman behind the wheel of the approaching car. The driver accelerated and sped past her toward the guarded gate, prompting the regal-looking Van Der Horst to yank her whistle from behind a picket sign and blow a shrill rebuke at the speeder she had once thought a friend and now called a scab.

At the start of the tenth week of the Eastern Airlines strike, workers seemed in good spirits as they picketed in front of the shuttle terminal at LaGuardia. As company vans transported out-of-town strike-breaking pilots and flight attendants from the Marriott Hotel, where many are being housed, to the shuttle terminal – virtually the only part of the company still flying – the picketers routinely let loose with whistles and catcalls. For those on the line, the worst week is over. State unemployment checks started arriving Saturday.

Van Der Horst, who has been a flight attendant at Eastern since 1959, is glad to have some cash in hand. "The first check won't even cover all of my car insurance bill. Next week's check is for my medical insurance. It's not much, but it helps." This might be the only positive development for Van Der Horst and her colleagues in this prolonged, tragic dispute. In ten weeks, the strike has all but receded from the front pages of the nation's newspapers, while the strikers have only become more bitter and determined.

"They're just trying to bleed us to death in the courts. Every day there's another delay," said Mike Pedano, who has refueled Eastern planes for nine years. As vans of scabs drove past the line, his voice became loud and angry. But when he stopped to talk privately about the strike, he spoke softly. "We lose if we win, and we lose if we lose," he said. "When we get back, everyone's going to be pointing the finger at everyone else, accusing this one of scabbing or that one of not doing enough. As far as the tight unit we once had, that's gone."

But more than just camaraderie has been lost. With Frank Lorenzo battling in bankruptcy court against creditors for the airline's carcass, the strike has been reduced to a long legal battle over who will try to revive the corpse. The strikers are well aware that even if a new buyer is found for Eastern, inevitably the carrier will be downscaled, many will lose their jobs, and thousands will be forced to return to work for lower wages.

In truth, that scenario is about the best Pedano and his fellow strikers can hope for. "We did succeed in beating Lorenzo," Pedano said, "but we destroyed our jobs at the same time." Still, most of the strikers believe they had no choice. Convinced that Lorenzo was breaking apart the company's assets anyway, they felt it necessary to take a stand. According to Pedano, "We all stood together, and we knew we'd face the consequences. But I just don't understand how he was allowed to get away with this, why Bush didn't step in. Lorenzo may walk away from this in good shape economically, but he's morally bankrupt and everyone knows it." It has come to this for the labor movement in America: fighting to get one owner to buy out another so that you can suffer lower wages and possible redundancy but somehow salvage your dignity.

Doubtless being morally right is preferable in the long run to being morally destitute, but there is something wrong in our country when the scales of justice seem to favor economic scavengers over those whose only crime is trying to earn an honest living . . .

Eastern Airlines picket line, postscript:
On June 8 1989, the Eastern Shuttle officially became the Trump Shuttle. The skies over the Northeast remain safe for corporate vultures.

ACROSS THE STREET is Woodlawn Cemetery, but all the ghosts cavort on this side of Bainbridge Avenue, in the seven-story building at 3555.

Since New York in the 1980s does a better job of housing phantoms and corpses than accomodating the still-breathing poor, it has become necessary during this housing famine to expose the hoarders of living space, their apologists in the media and their protectors in government, and to call the warehousing of apartments what it is: a disease of colossal greed.

Leon Calafiore, the president of the tenants' association at 3555, has lived in the building for ten years and remembers how easy it once was to get an apartment there. Rather suddenly, a few years ago, the landlord started refusing to rent when vacancies occurred. Just over a year ago, in March 1988, the building's owners, Hudson View Associates, filed a preliminary plan with the state attorney general's office to convert the building to a cooperative. The owners claimed that fewer than 10 percent of the sixty apartments were vacant. Legally, no more than 10 percent can be empty for five months before a co-op plan is submitted. This came as a surprise to the residents. "When we got our heads together, we realized the extent of the vacancy," Calafiore said. Tenants discovered that some 20 percent of the apartments had phantom residents, and four others were rented either to the superintendent or to his family members. The tenants' association fought back. It filed an affidavit challenging the landlord's numbers. The attorney general's office requested documentation from Hudson View Associates. Last month, the owners suddenly dropped their conversion plan.

Now, after a winter of heatless nights, more than a third of the building is empty: the demons of warehousing have run amok.

According to housing lawyer Michael Finder, situations like that on Bainbridge Avenue are not unusual. But it's not just the co-op conversions that produce warehousing. At Phipps Houses, an eight-building complex on prime real estate near 64th and Amsterdam, only 55 of 347 apartments are occupied, mostly by long-time elderly residents. Crack dealers regularly set up shop in empty units, scaring more tenants out.

Throughout the city, stories abound of empty apartments being kept off the market while a homeless population as high as 50,000 overflows city shelters and hotels. That is why, when you hear city housing chief Abe Biderman popping statistics at a council hearing with machine-gun speed to prove that the warehousing of apartments in New York is not a major problem, you just want to laugh . . .

As BEFITS THE Fort Knox of Wall Street, a vault that stores $3.5 trillion in stocks and bonds, the Depository Trust Company (DTC) usually keeps a very low profile.

Technically a bank, DTC was created by dozens of major Wall Street firms to track and record the daily trading of securities between individuals and companies. Last year alone 67 million transactions were tracked by the company and most new long-term municipal bonds are stored there. DTC employs 3,000 people just to figure out who owns all that paper wealth. Even with the aid of computers, accounting for so much paper is no easy job given the frantic daily trading of material and human capital perpetually on exhibit at the New York Stock Exchange.

Which brings us to our subject: the workers at DTC who keep this corporate vault running. Nearly 2,000 of these employees are members of Local 153 of the Office and Professional Employees International Union, and more than 60 percent of them are black, Hispanic or Asian. In the past year, these minority staffers have been complaining to management about their confinement in the DTC's basement, where they work as clerks, counters, janitors and secretaries. According to union leaders, black and Hispanic workers are concentrated in these lower-paying jobs (84 percent) while their white colleagues dominate the higher-paying jobs (54 percent). Arturo Antezana is a typical example. He started at DTC in 1967, and has worked for twenty-two years mostly as an intermediate clerk, for which he is now paid $23,000 a year. "I've watched dozens of whites with less experience than me promoted," he says, "and been denied promotions about twenty times." Justifiably angry, Antezana has gone through union grievance procedures and has filed a discrimination complaint against the company with the Equal Employment Opportunity Commission.

Company officials dispute claims of discrimination and insist that DTC has a good record of minority hiring. Tom Cardile, a senior vice president for human resources, points out that the ethnic and racial composition of the DTC workforce is close to that of the metropolitan area as a whole. As for promotions, Cardile insists that most occur from within the company. "We've got a pretty good mix in all of the classifications," he said. "Our numbers are very clean," added John Hahn, a director of personnel. "We look for the best-qualified employees to fill our internal positions. We hire anyone as long as they're qualified."

In recent months, union leaders Larry Mansour and Ed Jimenez have asked the Puerto Rican Legal Defense and Education Fund to represent the workers in the fight against DTC. As yet, there has been only one meeting between the lawyers for the two sides. The sad truth, however, is that workers who think they are victims of bias on the job cannot hope for much help from the judiciary, not with a Supreme Court packed with Reagan appointees working overtime to bury every employment-discrimination or affirmative-action case that comes before them.

If I were a corporate chief on Wall Street and I heard rumblings of discontent from the hundreds of blacks and Hispanics who handle $3.5 trillion of the Western world's wealth, I would – to put it mildly – be worried . . .

LAST WEEK, A pack of young white thugs chased young Yusuf Hawkins and his friends because they were black and had dared to enter the white neighborhood of Bensonhurst. One of the attackers gunned Hawkins down.

Years from now it will be written that the bullets that killed a 16-year-old black kid in Brooklyn on a warm August night in 1989 also finished off the career of Edward I. Koch. You knew it was the end of an era when the mayor of the city and the governor of the state sat down at Hawkins's funeral service in a small crowded Brooklyn church and listened to sermons from minister Louis Farrakhan and the Reverend Al Sharpton. You knew change was in the air when Ed Koch slipped out a back door to avoid reporters while David Dinkins, the man who could replace Koch as mayor, met the press afterwards and offered a message of unity and compassion . . .

"IT'S A BEAUTIFUL day," said Alyce Portia Fields, her frail body supported by a wooden cane as she emerged from the polling place on President Street in Crown Heights, Brooklyn. In the minds of this 95-year-old former schoolteacher and many others, September 12, 1989, is one for the history books. In central Brooklyn, black voters flocked to the polls in incredible numbers to pull the lever for David Dinkins in a mayoral primary race that became as polarized as any this city has seen.

In Crown Heights, where blacks and Hasidic Jews live in uneasy peace, the rift was as wide as Eastern Parkway. "I think he's been doing pretty good. He did pull the city out of bankruptcy" was how one Koch supporter defended the mayor. "We Jews are dumped on and pushed around just like the colored people. I have colored neighbors, we have no problems, but they just vote for Dinkins because of his skin."

In the mostly Puerto Rican 53rd Assembly District of Bushwick, the grand plan of Ed Koch to tip a close election by winning the Hispanic vote ran into trouble. "I like the black guy," said Juan Rios as he voted at Public School 123, a brown felt hat shading his aged, coppery face. "Remember when they killed Maria Hernandez?" he asked, referring to the anti-drug crusader gunned down by suspected dealers. "The black guy came here to support us. When they marched to the cemetery to bury her, he was right up front."

Back on President Street, Alyce Fields was in a philosophical mood: "God might have allowed all this Howard Beach and Bensonhurst stuff to happen so that it would open up the eyes of the people who couldn't see. Some of us are blind as bats, anyway."

Not so blind, it seems. On a day when more than 95 percent of the city's black voters rose as one to topple him, Edward I. Koch's act was over and New York politics will never be the same . . .

DEBORAH SILVA, curly-maned and copper-skinned, tried to keep her weight off her bad leg. On a day this important, the pain could wait. A half-dozen neighbors gathered around her outside of the Betances Houses for the elderly on St Anne's Avenue in the South Bronx. They lingered on the sidewalk in the warm autumn sun after depositing their votes inside. Silva was a very important senior citizen on this election day. A volunteer poll worker for David Dinkins, she could greet by first name nearly every person who came in to vote.

A tall, muscular young man carrying a Dinkins flyer stopped at the wall and kissed Silva on the cheek.

"Haven't seen you in a while," she smiled.

"I came to vote."

"Well, you know who the best man is," she said. The young man smiled and walked inside.

Silva feels strongly about this mayoral race. "At first I really liked Giuliani," she admitted. "But then he started all those attacks on Dinkins and everything got bitter. I'm older and understand these things. What are young people supposed to think when they see leaders setting those kinds of examples?" However, despite having lived in this country for twenty-two years, despite urging her friends and neighbors to support Dinkins, Silva is not a citizen and cannot cast a vote in this election. "I was born in Cuba," she explained. "My husband, Luis, was Puerto Rican; he always voted. He worked twelve years in the subways. Passed away six years ago . . . but the birthday cards kept coming."

"That happens a lot around here," said another woman. "Congressman Garcia always sends us birthday cards; in these projects everyone gets a card. We figured he must have gotten our birth dates from the voter lists. Even when you die, though, they don't stop."

"After the second year," Silvia added, "I went to Assemblyman Serrano's office and told the girl, 'Please ask Congressman Garcia to stop sending my husband's card.' They finally did."

A few blocks away, scores of Dinkins volunteers streamed in and out of a storefront office on Melrose Avenue, part of a massive people's movement to elect the first black mayor in the city's history. On St Anne's Avenue, though, an elderly widow, who was listed on no one's campaign payroll, leaned her arms against a brick wall and tried to nudge that history along. "Next year," Silva said, "I'm becoming a citizen. Not for any of the benefits. Just so I can vote." . . .

CRAIG AARON, in a blue sports coat with a black fez on his head, sat at the defense table in a fifth-floor courtroom in the Bronx yesterday.

The former Amtrak employee, devout Muslim, and eloquent tenant leader who had tried to rid his South Bronx building of drug dealers, was on trial for murder.

On the night of August 12, 1988, police were called to 2159 Morris Avenue and found a resident of the building, Larry Tyson, dead on a fourth-floor landing outside his apartment. Tyson had been stabbed thirty-one times in the neck, chest and back.

During the trial, the police testified that they found bloody sneaker tracks that led upstairs and ended outside Aaron's fifth-floor apartment and blood on Aaron's doorknob. When Aaron's girlfriend arrived and allowed them to enter the apartment, they saw blood on the floor and Aaron asleep. The police awakened Aaron and compared his sneaker to the footprints outside the apartment. The two did not match. Police found neither marks nor blood on him; there was no bloody clothing in the apartment, nor any possible murder weapon.

According to several neighborhood leaders, Tyson was a crack-head who allowed prostitutes to use his apartment, for a fee, as a place of business. Aaron, a dedicated local activist, had confronted Tyson a few times and had tried to get him to stop. "He was the only one willing to stand up to the dealers," said Catherine Von Kay, a resident of the block. "Everyone respected him."

On the night of his arrest, Aaron insisted that he knew nothing about Tyson's death and went with police to the 46th Precinct station, where he was questioned for a few hours and released. While he was being interrogated, police obtained a warrant to search his apartment and took samples of the blood in it. The next evening, as neighbors were in the middle of a block party Aaron had helped organize, he was arrested and charged with murder. Since then he has continued to maintain his innocence and rejected an offer from the district attorney to plea-bargain for manslaughter. Community leaders claim that neighbors who saw a group of young men running from the building around the time Tyson was killed are refusing to testify because they are afraid of the drug dealers in the building. They say residents of the floor where the slaying took place also are afraid.

The district attorney's office says it has one witness, now in jail, who says he saw Aaron commit the killing. Aaron's supporters say the witness was a friend of Tyson's. This person has yet to appear on the stand. The court audience has watched and listened as defense attorney Lewis Alperin grilled Detective Anthony Peregrin about his arrest of Aaron. Under Alperin's questioning, Peregrin admitted that the defendant's sneakers did not match the bloody footprints near the murder scene and that the defendant showed no signs of having been involved in a struggle.

"I don't believe he did this. I think the drug dealers just used this murder among themselves and figured they could get rid of Craig at the same time by blaming it on him" was the opinion of another resident of the block who has known Aaron for years.

There remains the unresolved question of how blood got inside Aaron's apartment. But we must consider, as well, the continuing terror that drug dealers have imposed on the neighborhoods of this city and ask: What are decent people supposed to do when the law can't protect them? How should one respond when just saying "no" isn't enough? . . .

CONSIDER THE FOLLOWING items of teen consumer news: In his video-taped confession, accused Central Park jogger rapist Raymond Santana recounted how he and a mob of teenagers once attacked a male jogger to steal his Walkman radio. After discovering the Walkman had no cassette player, they tossed it in the trash. "Nobody wants just a radio anymore," said Santana.

The woman we'll call Elaine Matos couldn't believe it when Robert walked into her office with only socks on.

"Where are your shoes?"

"Somebody stole my L.A. Gears."

"Don't you have any other shoes to wear?" the counselor asked the 16-year-old Brooklynite who lives in her agency's group home.

"Aw, Miss Matos, I ain't wearing those old Converses — the other kids will laugh at me."

It seems that we have reached a point in city life where a teenager will choose to walk the streets barefoot before being caught in out-of-style sneakers, where poor children go to school wearing enough gold on their necks or teeth to keep South Africa's mines working overtime and their own young lives in danger . . .

AT FIRST GLANCE, the three-story brick building at 66 Whipple Street looks abandoned, like most of the buildings on this desolate block in Williamsburg, Brooklyn. Inside, however, Carmen Nieves, Miguel DeJesus and many others are waging the kind of fight that used to make Americans proud to be called workers.

A long time ago, if you belonged to a labor union it meant you'd won the battle for respect: you couldn't be fired just because the boss didn't like you; you earned a decent wage, even something called overtime; and anyone who wanted to work you into the ground had to pay time-and-a-half for the privilege. In the America of the 1990s, however, many of these labor safeguards have been jackhammered to bits by greed. If the trend continues, the CEOs, the bankers and their lawyers will litter this country with the broken bones of the labor movement — except for those crippled unions that do exactly as they're told.

Which brings me to the 5,000 garment workers, 80 percent of whom are Hispanic, who toil in the 150 member factories of the Williamsburg Trade Association. Until recently, all of these workers were represented in a joint contract with the factory owners by Local 17–18 of the United Production Workers, an outfit formed in 1974 (the same year as the trade association). According to the people at 66 Whipple Street, Local 17–18 is not a member of the AFL–CIO, has never had an election or called a strike since its founding, and rarely files grievances or seeks arbitration. They say 17–18 is a company union which has been selling them out to the association from the start. The list of grievances is lengthy and persuasive. For example, one of the dissidents, Nieves, worked for several years on a blindstitch machine at an association factory on Spencer Street. She recalls how two years ago, in January 1988, she went into the hospital for an operation, only to find out that she had no health insurance because the company hadn't paid the premiums. It took Nieves eight months of fighting with Local 17–18 leaders – who are paid to be on top of these things – to get her bills covered.

Nieves, though, is lucky: she's a citizen who speaks English and isn't afraid to fight. Most of the workers in the piecework sweatshops are Mexican, Dominican or Haitian immigrants who speak no English. A good number are in this country illegally and are afraid to protest abuses. Miguel DeJesus, a Dominican immigrant and former presser at Mademoiselle, said he always worked nine-hour days with no overtime.

These workers now want the International Ladies' Garment Workers Union to represent them. Last week, ILGWU organizers filed 1,500 signatures requesting new elections in more than two dozen factories. The union, reeling from a huge loss in membership as the garment industry flees New York for cheap labor markets in the South and the Far East, has mounted its most ambitious union drive in decades in Williamsburg. And because most of the workers live in the area, the ILGWU has won the support of many local community organizations and churches.

Jonathan Charm, executive director of the trade association which represents the owners, called the number of signatures filed Thursday "very small." "They're great at flinging mud," he said of the ILGWU, "but the workers have rejected them. They're looking for new blood to suck. The reason there is no garment industry left in New York is because the ILGWU has priced labor out of competition."

Ironic but typical: workers who make as little as $3.50 an hour, who can be fired at a moment's notice despite having union representation, are being warned not to price themselves out of competition. Every boss I ever worked for, whenever the subject of labor came up, would cry that while he was losing money or not making enough, his employees kept asking for more, more, more – and then his crocodile tears would flow all the way to the bank. Only difference is, in the old days, nobody was fooled . . .

No. 369 WALKED over from the tree, past the line of chattering women seated on empty plastic milk cartons, and squatted between no. 7 and no. 162. He wore beat-up light brown shoes, no socks, and spoke in broken English. It was near noon on a hot July day in 1990. Soon they would all move out from under the shade of the plant's walls and begin walking in circles, clutching placards, under the torrid sun.

About 100 feet down Kent Avenue, through a gap between two factories, you can gaze past the Williamsburg waterfront and see the twin towers of the World Trade Center rising above the sweltering haze of lower Manhattan. To appreciate those shimmering skyscrapers and the legions of well-dressed office workers inside them who peck away at computer terminals and keep track of the world's money, one must also understand the human foundation of immigrant labor, abused and forgotten, on which so much of the glitter rests.

For six months now, two hundred employees of the Domsey Trading Corporation have been on the picket line, striking for the right to have a union. They include no. 369 (Jean Bonny), no. 7 (Giles Robinson), and no. 162 (Adrian Castillo). I refer to them by their numbers because that is how they are known to the bosses at Domsey. For years these workers have been identified only by the numerals printed on the plastic tags pinned to their chests.

Domsey is a company that buys clothing and furniture from charitable groups such as the Salvation Army and Goodwill Industries and then sorts, packages and resells it, mostly in Africa. In addition to reducing its workers to mere numbers, Domsey has also denied them the right to pick their own union representation. The employees, tired of being treated as less than human, are out on the line – forcing the company to take them and their concerns into account. The grievances are many and longstanding; Domsey has had a chequered history when it comes to labor relations. Over the years, a succession of unions represented the workers until the last one, Local 113, was removed by the courts following a legal dispute. According to the workers, when that happened, owner Arthur Salm and his sons, Peter and Cliff, who manage the plant, stopped paying overtime and most holidays, canceled the health insurance policy, and began treating the workforce more harshly.

Now, workers who forget to wear their tags are fined $5 or sent home without pay. "I've worked in that plant for two years and nobody has ever known my name," Bonny explained. "They always say, '369 come here!' or '369 do this!' Each day in there I feel humiliated." It's a humiliation he's had to bear. Sorting used clothes for $145 a week is the only job 33-year-old Bonny's had since coming to the US from Haiti. His folks back home, his wife and three kids, all need the $50 a week he sets aside for them. With the other $95, Bonny manages to survive in this city.

Robinson – no. 7 – was a little better off before the strike. After twenty-seven years as a number, he was making $7.45 an hour. "When I started, it was mostly Puerto Ricans and black Americans," he recalled. "Neither of us would take much stuff. We knew our rights. Later, the boss started bringing in Haitians and Dominicans – I was one of the last Americans left."

Last year, Robinson began a campaign to bring the International Ladies' Garment Workers Union into the plant. He was fired from Domsey on the very day the union filed a petition for recognition with the National Labor Relations Board. This was in December. It took one month for the situation to reach breaking point. On January 30, the workers walked out after another union activist was dismissed. The NLRB has ruled their action an unfair labor practice strike – in other words, a walkout caused not by economic demands but by an employer's attempts to prevent union organization.

The strike has turned nasty over the last six months. First the company brought in replacement workers, a.k.a. scabs, thereby adopting the classic 1980s corporate method for conquering worker unrest. The Salms, though, added a new twist by hiring prisoners on work-release to sort the clothes — that is, until the union complained to the state Correctional Services Department. At present, New York law forbids using prisoners for strikebreaking, but how long this law will last in our anti-union era is anybody's guess.

The NLRB has filed a laundry list of complaints against both management and the union for physical assaults and harassment. Until hearings are held and these complaints are resolved, the board can't hold an election. The Brooklyn director of the NLRB admits these charges could tie up the conflict indefinitely and "play into the hands of the employer," but his hands are tied as well.

No. 369, who came from Haiti to earn $145 a week in New York City packing used clothes for Africa within plain sight of Wall Street, stared at the plant with a confident, determined expression. "I believe in American justice," he said. "Sooner or later, we will have our election. They will lose." . . .

THIS CITY'S MOST spendthrift politicians could take a few lessons from Brooklyn College student Jean LaMarre.

In his position as chairman of the City University of New York's student senate, LaMarre represents 200,000 mostly poor and working-class students struggling to stay in college despite escalating tuition costs. But during the past year, while protests and strikes against tuition hikes rocked the university, LaMarre went on a bit of a spending spree. The extraordinary expenses charged to the student senate, a group composed of representatives from CUNY's student governments, included:

- $13,000 for limousines to transport LaMarre and a handful of other student officers around town;

- $49,000 for a three-day student legislative lobbying conference in Albany in February, of which $24,000 was spent on room service;
- $2,200 for electronic pagers;
- $24,000 for LaMarre's full-time personal assistant, Elizabeth, who is also his twin sister;
- $26,000 for a weekend conference at Lake Placid;
- $500 for a speech given by City Council candidate Adam Clayton Powell V at a student senate conference in August, less than a month before the primary election;
- $300 for a watercolor painting to hang in the student senate office;
- $300 for a new sign with 30-inch "satin finished gold acrylic letters" to hang outside the senate office;
- $1,000 for airfare for LaMarre, Elizabeth and another student to travel to Montreal for a "conference site search";
- $7,700 for the rental of twenty-nine walkie-talkies for a student rally. This was high because LaMarre and his officers did not return the walkie-talkies for several weeks;
- $4,500 in legal fees for several students arrested for scuffling with police in Albany last spring when students led by LaMarre broke away from a larger budget protest organized by the Black and Puerto Rican Legislative Caucus;
- $4,500 for Elizabeth and two others to attend an African American summit in Africa. There was no documentation of how the money was spent.

"It doesn't take a rocket scientist to figure out spending that kind of money on a car service doesn't do anybody any good, including the person who took the ride," commented one CUNY official, who asked not to be identified. Well, young LaMarre may not find work with NASA, but from where I sit, he sure looks made for City Council . . .

*

JOSEPH RIVERA MATOS was three weeks old on April 6, 1973, when his mother, Sonia, took him to a clinic at Bronx Lebanon Hospital for a "missile shot," the combination vaccination against diphtheria, pertussis and tetanus.

The next day Sonia called her husband, Victor, at work. The baby had just had a seizure, was running a high fever, and wouldn't wake up. The Matoses rushed Joseph to the now-defunct, city-owned Fordham Hospital. "The doctors put him in ice and he suddenly woke up," Victor recalls. "Then they told us we could take him home." According to papers filed in the US Claims Court, the staff at Fordham had given the infant a spinal tap, diagnosed a viral infection, and sent him home with a prescription for phenobarbital. Two days later Joseph had another seizure. By the time his parents got him to Fordham, his temperature was 105°. The nurses told them that there were no empty beds and transferred the feverish infant to Misericordia Hospital by ambulance. When Victor and Sonia took him home two months later, the doctors mentioned some complicated term, "diffuse encephalopathy, probably secondary to pertussis."

In other words, something had gone wrong with the vaccine.

Joseph will turn twenty next month. He is handsome and basically healthy, with thick curly black hair and sparkling eyes. But he cannot walk, talk or understand what is said to him. He must be bathed and spoonfed as he is unable to control his arms. He will wear Pampers for the rest of his life because he cannot control his bodily functions. If he is hungry, in pain or upset, there is no way for him to tell his father, and he spends his days crawling about his Bronx apartment uttering unintelligible sounds.

During the first few years, his parents, who are natives of Puerto Rico, had no idea that they could sue the hospitals involved. They did not know that their son was part of a tiny group of children in this country who have had severe adverse reactions to vaccines for diphtheria and polio. In 1976, when they learned they were not alone, the Matoses filed suit in Bronx Supreme Court against the city, the Health and Hospitals Corporation and Bronx Lebanon. They were represented by Preston Douglas. Seventeen years later, Douglas is still their lawyer and the case is still lumbering through the courts. Joseph Rivera and his family have yet to see a single penny of compensation for what has been an unspeakably difficult life for all of them. No money for lost earnings, rehabilitation, or nursing care. Nothing.

Not that Joseph's illness has been the family's only problem. When the boy was five, his parents separated. Victor, then the owner of a couple of buildings and grocery stores, shot a man dead in self-defense. He beat a manslaughter charge but did twenty-two months for illegal gun possession. By the time Victor got out of prison, Sonia, now his estranged wife, had disappeared with Joseph and their daughter. He tracked her down. When Sonia died in 1986, Victor regained custody of his children.

Nineteen eighty-six was also the year Congress passed the National Childhood Vaccine Injury Act. It was intended to protect the companies that produced the immunization vaccines and the medical providers who administered them from whopping court settlements. In 1988, the federal government agreed to pay compensation for children who were killed or severely damaged by immunization programs. Since then, more than 4,000 cases have been settled by the US Claims Court under the act, with awards averaging nearly $1 million. But there's a catch: to be eligible under the federal program, a plaintiff must voluntarily drop any legal action in local courts. In 1989, Bronx Lebanon moved for a summary judgment of the Matos case; when neither Victor nor his lawyer appeared for the hearing, the judge dismissed the suit and recommended that the family seek compensation from the federal government. However, because the case had been dismissed involuntarily instead of voluntarily – a legal technicality – Joseph was ruled ineligible for the federal program by a US magistrate.

When I called the family's lawyer, Douglas, to get more information on this mix-up, he refused to talk to me, as did lawyers from Bronx Lebanon and the Health and Hospitals Corporation. From the case record, I learned that Douglas got Bronx Supreme Court Judge Douglas McKeon to vacate the original 1989 Bronx dismissal last June. He then filed a new appeal with the US Claims Court, which ordered the federal magistrate to hold a new hearing on Joseph's case six months ago.

Maybe by the time he's twenty-five or thirty-five, this country's insane judicial system will finally give Joseph Matos the consideration he deserves . . .

BERNADETTE POWELL was already an inmate at Bedford Hills Correctional Facility on March 10, 1980. That was the night jilted socialite educator Jean Harris, overcome by jealous rage, pumped four bullets into her lover, diet doctor Herman Tarnower, and plunged Scarsdale's lordly residents into the gutters of a crime scandal unmatched since gangster Bugsy Siegel cavorted there half a century ago. The Super Bowl of society trials followed. The details of the affair between the haughty girls' school headmistress and the aging playboy were exposed in court and devoured by the press. Harris and her money's-no-object lawyers mounted a relentless defense. They spent years in appeals and motions for new trials that went all the way to the US Supreme Court.

A year after Tarnower's murder, Harris entered Bedford Hills to begin serving a sentence of fifteen years to life. There, she joined fellow inmate Powell, a poor black woman from Binghamton who had been convicted of the same crime of second-degree murder and who had been slapped with the same fifteen-to-life sentence for shooting her ex-husband.

Powell's case never made the national press. It barely got out of Binghamton.

Like so many women in jail for murder, Powell had been a victim of physical abuse by the man she killed. Over a four-year period, her husband had beaten her, forced her to stand under scalding hot water in a shower, even locked her in the trunk of his car. After their divorce, she obtained numerous orders of protection that he routinely violated. In July 1978, in the midst of a custody fight over their 4-year-old son, he pushed her and the boy into his car at gunpoint and took them to a motel in Ithaca. There, Bernadette Powell shot and killed him. She claimed self-defense. Prosecutors offered her a plea bargain: a four-year sentence for criminally negligent homicide. She refused. The prosecutor, who had once been accused of beating his wife, won a quick conviction for second-degree murder. Unlike Harris, Powell had no expensive lawyers. She made do with a court-appointed attorney.

In jail, Powell became a library clerk, a model prisoner and a student at Mercy College. Five nights a week for four years, she attended classes and maintained a 3.8 grade-point average. In 1985, at the age of thirty-three, she received a Bachelor of Arts degree, summa cum laude. While Powell took honors for her studies, Harris did what she had done all her life – she taught. The only difference was that her students in Binghamton were hard-bitten inmates instead of dainty debutantes.

Some years back, Powell became the subject of a book, *Everyday Death*. It was written by Ann Jones, who has made a crusade of getting justice for battered women. Powell's case became a *cause célèbre* for battered women's groups and a Bernadette Powell Defense Committee was established. With all her appeals exhausted by 1985, Powell's only hope for early release was clemency from Governor Cuomo. For years now, she has appealed to him.

Yesterday, on December 30, 1992, Mario Cuomo granted clemency to a jilted woman who wouldn't let her lover go, but not to a woman whose ex-husband wouldn't leave her alone. Jean Harris, that rare jailbird from the ranks of the rich, leaves Bedford Hills under the same spotlight and fanfare with which she entered. But Bernadette Powell, an example thousands of young black and Latino mothers in jail could emulate, remains behind bars, lost for thirteen years in the shadows of a justice that is anything but blind . . .

*

PATRICK MOORE was the last mourner to leave grave no. 11776. His mother, Linda, her eyes clenched shut with pain, had sought refuge in one of the waiting black limousines. Two of his aunts, wailing inconsolably, had collapsed on the damp ground and been carried away from the gravesite. The crowd of family, friends and reporters had departed for the line of parked cars. Only Patrick, a gangly young man in an immaculate black suit and gold earring, remained. He couldn't stop staring into the open grave that now held the body of his brother, Ian.

On the morning of December 12, 1992, Ian, aged seventeen, and Tyrone Sinkler, aged sixteen, were shot to death by a classmate at Thomas Jefferson High School. Their violent deaths stunned, momentarily, this homicide-numbed city. Yesterday afternoon, Ian was laid to rest in Brooklyn's Evergreen Cemetery after a funeral service in East New York at which David Dinkins tried to make sense of these tragic losses and expressed genuine outrage at the city's ever-expanding killing fields.

On the other side of Brooklyn, in a federal courtroom, a murder of another kind was being examined as one-time Gambino family underboss Salvatore (Sammy the Bull) Gravano fingered John Gotti, the godfather, for masterminding the 1985 steakhouse assassination of Paul Castellano. For the past few days, Gotti and Gravano, vicious gangsters and dope traffickers from another era, have captured the city's crime-obsessed imagination.

But it is the cold-blooded assassination of two teenagers *in a public school* for no apparent reason that speaks more to the future of our city than a tired turf fight among a bunch of gangsters. After all, Gravano admits to nineteen killings in twenty years; Jefferson's principal, Carol Burt-Beck, has seen fifty of her students murdered during the past five.

Two crime stories from the borough of Brooklyn: one of murder in the New York that was, the other of genocide in the city we are fast becoming . . .

*

WHEN HIS DAUGHTER Shalimar was jumped and beaten by nine teenagers on the D train in Brooklyn coming home from Edward R. Murrow High School on December 6, 1991, Roberto de la Torre made her file a complaint with transit police. That was seven months ago and, although a friend of the 16-year-old identified one of the attackers, no one has been arrested.

Then it happened again. Last month, Shalimar and a friend were boarding the D train at the M Street station when a burly young man punched her in the chest and yanked two gold chains from her neck. Afterwards, the honors student told her father she would rather drop out and get a general equivalency diploma than risk being killed on the train to school. No way, said de la Torre. He felt he had no choice but to meet his daughter after school and escort her home.

This was no easy task for a postal worker whose wife also works full-time. De la Torre leaves the house at 3:30 each morning and walks seventeen blocks to catch a train so that he can reach his mid-town Manhattan post office by 6 A.M. To return to Brooklyn in time to meet Shalimar, de la Torre decided to split his annual vacation into two-hour chunks to be taken daily. Soon he was shepherding Shalimar's friends home, too. In New York City today, thousands of children live with the very real fear of not making it home from school alive.

Even with her stocky father beside her, Shalimar did not find the commute a smooth ride. On May 29, as the subway pulled out of the crowded Kings Highway station, de la Torre, Shalimar and her friends were surrounded by a mob of thirty or more rowdy teenagers who were cursing and harassing passengers. Still in his blue mailman's uniform, de la Torre suggested strongly to the loudmouths that they quiet down.

"We kill mailmen, motherfucker," one of them said as the teens reached into their knapsacks for something more than pencils.

De la Torre got between his kids and the gang and reached into his jacket, pretending he had a gun. Despite his bravado, the gang mugged and robbed several other passengers. When the train reached the next stop, de la Torre grabbed the door and screamed for the cops, but the hoodlums fled before help arrived.

Regular classes are over now. Shalimar is taking her Regents' exams and de la Torre is back on his normal shift. In September, his younger daughter, Shaileen, will attend Murrow. By then her father's vacation time will be just about used up. "I want to get my licence and get a car," Shalimar said. "I just don't want to go through this again, or my sister, either." Now, de la Torre will have to find a way to pay for the car and the insurance so his daughters can go to school without fear.

This Sunday, Father's Day, the de la Torre family will celebrate those family values that Dan Quayle claims have been lost in the inner city . . .

IN MAY OF 1988, two home improvement salesmen from Harbor Crest Associates Ltd. showed up on the doorstep of widow Caroline Berger's bungalow in Roosevelt, Long Island and wouldn't take no for an answer. Berger told them she was on a fixed income and couldn't afford any repairs. Legally blind and wheelchair-bound, she is at age sixty-six the sole provider for her retarded granddaughter, Rita, and Rita's daughter, Carolyn, who is afflicted with cerebral palsy. From her late husband's pension and Supplemental Security Income payments for Rita and Carolyn, she gets a total of $1,800 a month. Berger has no savings in the bank. "I never had credit . . . [but] they talked like it wasn't nothing," she said of their 100 percent financing offer.

Before she knew it, Berger had agreed to a $5,800 job that included vinyl siding, three storm doors, new gutters and trim. The salesmen gave her some papers to sign, a few of which were blank. (Only later, according to documents on file in the US District Court, Eastern District, did she discover that someone had stuck a 1 in front of the 5, changing her bill to $15,800.) Six days after she signed the agreement, the salesmen returned and talked her into a new roof and sewer hookup for $9,800. Then there were two more contracts – for a 10-by-15-foot deck ($8,800) and cyclone fencing ($9,350). The deck off the side of the house remains an especially puzzling addition. No door leads on to it, so Berger must maneuver herself down the bungalow's front steps, have someone wheel her along the side alley, and then drag herself up the deck stairs while someone lifts the wheelchair on to it. The most incredible contract of all was dated February 14, 1989. It instructed Harbor Crest to remove Berger's newly installed vinyl siding and replace it with vinyl brickette. The firm also replaced one of the new storm doors. All this for an additional $14,700!

Within a year, the widow had fallen $49,700 into debt. Each new contract brought more monthly payment books from finance companies like Sterling Resources Ltd. and Dartmouth Plan Inc. Unbeknownst to Berger, the loans were secured by second mortgages on her house that were then sold to banks. Her payments climbed to $838, nearly half of her monthly income.

According to a civil class-action racketeering suit now before chief US District Judge Thomas Platt, Berger is just one of at least two dozen poor, black, elderly women who got caught in a complex trap set by fraudulent contractors and finance companies. Last Friday, Platt granted a motion to begin discovery proceedings into the case.

Bessie McKay, forty-four years old, a single parent from Freeport, has already signed an affidavit. She suffers from diabetes, asthma and a brain tumor and claims she was a classic victim of a Harbor Crest swindle. In 1986, she was pressured into signing a $1,900 contract to remodel her 6-by-6-foot kitchen, a job which she claims was poorly done. But the contract for which the salesman secured financing listed a $19,800 bill, although McKay had kept a copy of the original $1,900 contract. No one would listen to her at Harbor Crest, and no one ever told her that she had mortgaged her house. All McKay got was a cheap kitchen and a payment book with $335-a-month coupons. Naturally, it didn't take her long to fall behind on payments, and in 1988 McKay was evicted from the home she had lived in for nine years.

Attorney Harry Kutner has located more than two dozen home-owners who fit a similar pattern: a black, elderly widow or single woman with little education, from a low-income neighborhood of Long Island. All were pressured to sign legal papers for contracts they couldn't possibly afford; none of them were ever told that in doing so they were signing a mortgage on their homes. According to Kutner, hundreds of homeowners in Long Island, Brooklyn and Queens may have been victimized by the same scam. In papers filed last week, one of the banks involved, Bank Atlantic of Fort Lauderdale, said it has already started foreclosure of mortgages for thirty homes that were originally contracted by Harbor Crest. Harbor Crest, it transpires, has since closed up shop.

Jerry Reisman is an attorney for Sterling Resources Ltd., a finance company named in the suit. He insists the allegations of a racketeering conspiracy have no merit. "Sterling solely purchased the paper from the contractors," Reisman said. "In most instances it appears that the homeowners could make the payments."

His argument may not stand up in court. Just last month, the *New York Times* reported that Bay Banks, Inc. in Boston agreed to a multi-million-dollar settlement for 11,000 low-income homeowners who were misled by home improvement contractors operating with the approval of the bank.

Home repair scams could be a trend – open season on poor, elderly widows as the economy gets meaner . . .

THE FOUR CON ED workers had done everything by the book as they repaired a gas line in East New York. So Jimmy Egan, the team's 63-year-old safety specialist, was a little surprised when he found himself flat on his back with the steel tip of his work boot stuck in his face — and his foot still in it. He never saw the car turn on to Crescent Street and bounce like a toy off the oncoming lumber truck. Egan was blind-sided by a mass of steel that plowed past the safety barriers his team had erected, crushing him against a van.

That was on a brilliant September morning last year. Nine months later, Egan is still trying to secure permanent disability benefits from a company that annually gives out millions of dollars in executive bonuses for, among other things, keeping down death and injury claims by its employees.

There are 13,000 workers in Local 1–2 of Utility Workers of America. Over the years they've had a work-related death and injury rate that rivals that of the New York Police Department. Four died on the job last year, another four in 1990, three in 1989. The number of injured each year is in the hundreds. "I saw a fellow on Vernon Boulevard come out of a manhole once with no clothes on," Egan said. "The fire from an explosion had burned all his clothes off." And then there are the other health hazards. "I remember years ago we played in asbestos," Egan recalled. "Nobody told us it was dangerous back then. We'd throw it on guys." Today, union leaders say one of every ten Con Ed workers shows signs of asbestosis or asbestos-related cancer.

These sacrifices are important to remember this weekend, when we will be hearing a lot of nasty threats to its unionized workforce from Con Edison – a company which collected $5.9 billion in revenues and then gave its shareholders (not to be confused with its customers) $530 million in profits out of all those nasty little blue and white bills they send us each month. In fact, Con Edison has gotten so good at giving out money that last year it gave out nearly $4 million in bonuses to 400 management employees. Some of the bonuses were as much as 15 percent of the managers' salaries, and they rewarded, according to confidential company memos, some unusual accomplishments:

- One lawyer in the company's asbestos defense team got a bonus for managing to settle two asbestos death court cases "for $2,000 each at the commencement of jury selection," while plaintiffs who went to trial received settlements of $900,000;
- A public relations manager got a bonus for confusing and muzzling the press during the Gramercy Park explosion;

• A Washington lobbyist was given a bonus for getting Congress to ease some federal pollution requirements against the company.

Admittedly, companies have a right to give out bonuses for whatever reason they choose; however, in the past Con Ed has done so from its profits. Now, the company has persuaded the state Public Service Commission to allow it to pay these bonuses out of revenues from its customers. And all of this would not be so interesting if Con Edison had not announced this week – at the beginning of the summer peak demand period – that it is prepared to lock out its 13,000 union workers and operate only with management personnel unless the unions agree to a new contract by midnight Saturday. While the union members have authorized a strike, they say that they are prepared to keep talking after the deadline.

The managers who put together the strike contingency plan will undoubtedly be first in line for this year's customer-funded bonuses . . .

ON THE MORNING of July 3, 1992, Karen Messinger was about to turn off the television and head off to work at the General Motors auto plant in North Tarrytown when President Bush came on. A reporter was asking Bush to explain how 10 million people looking for work was a sign that things in this country are improving. For Messinger, a pipe fitter at the GM plant who in two weeks will say goodbye to 850 departing fellow workers, this was a timely question that stopped her in her tracks.

The president said something about good news and bad news. The good news, according to Bush, was that the Federal Reserve Bank had dropped the discount rate to 3 percent. And the bad news – the government's announcement of the highest unemployment rate since 1983 – would disappear in short order, Bush predicted, as he criticized all the naysayers.

"It seemed he was saying that if we all think positive like

Tinkerbell, everything will be all right," Messinger said, shaking her head in disbelief.

Just as there was no way to whitewash Bush's vomiting all over the Japanese prime minister, there is no way the Republicans can clean up the ugly unemployment stats less than two weeks before the Democrats gather at Madison Square Garden. That's why the Federal Reserve jumped faster than a baseball off a Mark McGwire bat to drop the discount rate by half a point. (The last time the Fed rate was that low, Jack Kennedy was romping in the White House with John-John and Caroline.)

Obviously, this desperate action by the Fed is meant to get the economy cranked up before the election in November. And, of course, it will do nothing of the kind. Anyone lucky enough to have a savings account knows that banks are paying next to nothing to hold your money while demanding such loanshark rates on credit-card balances that you could drive a GM truck in a drunken stupor between one rate and the other. The lower rates may give the banks more spread regarding profits and may even encourage some businessmen to take out more loans with which to buy newer machines and lay off more workers. But they will convince few American consumers to take on more debts. As for buying a house or a car, not a chance. So many people go to bed at night not knowing if their jobs will be around in six months that the interest rate could be zero and they still wouldn't bite.

At the GM plant in North Tarrytown, the Fed's generosity has certainly fallen on deaf ears. Messinger remembers how, two years ago, "management told us all to go out and buy cars and houses because our jobs were secure." She bought property in Peekskill. But then GM decided to lay off 75,000 workers nationwide and announced that Tarrytown and dozens of other plants would be closed by 1995. Now Messinger wonders how she'll pay her mortgage.

Actually it is her friends' and coworkers' mortgages which Messinger is most concerned about. Even though she has worked for the plant for fewer than eight years, her job is safe for now because she's a skilled worker. But as secretary-treasurer of United Auto Workers Local 664, she deals on a daily basis with the frustrations of those who aren't so lucky. When the plant shuts for summer retooling on July 17, the second shift will be eliminated and workers with as much as ten years' seniority will be sent packing. "Where are you going to find a production job that pays $17.50 an hour?" Messinger asks. "Most of the people will either have to find much lower-paying jobs if they can, or try to move somewhere else, chasing GM jobs like nomads." Transfers from other GM plants are called GM gypsies or Document 28s, after a section in the union contract. Some have been laid off from as many as five different plants. One of Messinger's friends, Cynthia Matthews, is a Document 28. Matthews moved to Tarrytown after getting laid off from the GM plant in Norwood, Ohio. Now she will be laid off again.

Of course, GM employees are not alone. The itinerant worker has become a regular feature of downsized American industry. In a couple of weeks, 500 Taystee workers in Queens will lose their jobs. In New Jersey, a few thousand state workers will soon hit the bricks. Over in California, where the unemployment rate is the highest in the nation, defense contractors are releasing workers by the thousands. American companies keep fleeing to Mexico and Taiwan and Singapore, always insisting that American labor costs too much. The products that come back, however, never cost less, although workers forced into lower-paying jobs are expected to keep buying.

This country is in an economic free fall, and the people in the White House have no idea what to do. For decades, the Cold War fueled a gargantuan military complex that gobbled up our tax dollars but at least provided millions of jobs. Now the Cold War is over, and Tinkerbell can't help . . .

THE TWO-PARAGRAPH, typewritten letter is filled with misspellings and grammatical errors. Like most racist venom, it is anonymous.

GREETINGS TO ALL MEMBERS OF THE BLUE ORDER.
CONGRADULATIONS ARE DUE FOR THE JOB DONE ON DARREN
PANNELL. SOME SUCCESS HAS BEEN MADE IN GETTING RID OF
LATIMORE GUESS HE BE GOING BACK TO THE CHICKEN FARM. NEXT
ASSIGNMENT WILL BE LLOYD FINLEY, ERIC ADAMS AND THE
GUARDIANS. AFTER THEY FALL THE REST WILL BE EASY.

KEEP YOUR EYES AND HEARS OPEN YOU ARE OUR STRENTH!
THE BLUE ORDER

Hand-delivered in early December 1992 to the mailboxes of more than two dozen white transit cops in Manhattan's District 1 command at Columbus Circle and signed with a swastika, the letter congratulated the white Brooklyn transit cops who shot fellow black officer Derwin Pannell on the evening of November 11 – an "accidental death" which is still under investigation – and fingers the department's highest-ranking black commander, Deputy Chief George Latimer, and the leaders of the fraternity organization of black cops, Lloyd Finley and Eric Adams.

A crackpot note like this would normally be thrown away without further ado. In this case, however, copies of the letter were distributed inside a police station where, transit brass admit, hostilities between black and white officers have been simmering for more than a year. District 1 has been racially polarized ever since Michael Gordon, a fast-rising black lieutenant, was accused of supplying information to black cops on the 1991 sergeant's exam. Anger over the sergeant's exam controversy sparked fistfights between black and white officers. Three cops, including Gordon, were eventually indicted by the Manhattan DA on misdemeanor charges, but their cases have not yet come to trial.

According to black officers on the force, the shooting of Pannell last month by two of his fellow transit cops who mistook him for a mugger has made a bad situation worse. The black officers' fraternal group, the Grand Council of Guardians, has increasingly come under fire from white members of the force for being too outspoken, too powerful. Eric Adams, the Guardians' spokesman, has been threatened numerous times during the past year, sometimes in rather odd ways. A dead fish was mailed in a Zip-lock plastic bag to his police desk; a dead rat glued to a rat tray was left on the hood of his car.

The Blue Order letter was stumbled upon by a young black transit cop while he was checking his mail slot at the back of the muster area. "I thought maybe somebody forgot to put a letter in my cubby hole," explained the officer, who had reached into a fellow officer's box to eyeball what he thought was a routine announcement. When he read it, he was stunned. Then he noticed the envelopes had only been placed in white cops' boxes. "I couldn't believe that it's come to a situation like this" was his emotional reply.

A mixture of common sense and wishful thinking would have you believe that the letter is the work of one demented mind. If the cop who found the letter is to be believed, however, more than two dozen of his fellow officers received personally addressed copies – and a week later none of them has reported it to Internal Affairs.

"My name was on it," Adams said. "Do I believe there is a white supremacist organization inside law enforcement?" Adams asked. "Based on the information I'm receiving, yes." I talked with him several times by telephone last weekend. Yesterday morning, when I walked downstairs from my Bronx apartment to my car, I found that someone had left a dead rat, glued to a rat tray, on my front hood.

A week later, a different station, a second racist memo. Police Sergeant Art Williams received the flyer in a plain white envelope that was personally addressed to him at the Manhattan traffic area precinct on West 30th Street. In big bold letters, the flyer said:

YOU HAVE BEEN CHOSEN TO COMPETE WITH OTHER FINALISTS FOR THE PLANNED SEQUEL TO PLANET OF THE APES. BRING YOUR KINKY HAIR, FAT LIPS, FLAT NOSE AND BLACK ASS TO 143 W. 44th St., ON MONDAY DECEMBER 14, 1992 AT 10:00 AM (C.P.TIME); (8:00 AM FOR ALL OTHER RACES.)

At first, Williams, who is black and a 24-year veteran of the force, thought it was a tasteless joke — after all, the address in the flyer doesn't exist. Then he learned that his driver, Officer James Forbes, who also is black, had received the same letter the night before and that Duane Montgomery, another black sergeant in the traffic division who works out of 1 Police Plaza, had also been sent a copy. That's when all three realized that this was something more than sick humor — race hate, pure and simple, from within police ranks.

When Williams heard about the goings-on at District 1, he became enraged. "When I read about that Blue Order, I realized racist stuff like this is serious," Williams said. "There's got to be a stop to this trash."

All three officers have reported the letters to police internal affairs investigators. Meanwhile, transit police internal affairs and FBI agents who have stepped in to investigate the Blue Order letter have so far been unable to find any copies other than the one turned over to me by the black officer who asked to remain anonymous.

The Blue Order may turn out to be a community of one or two raving lunatics, but the question of racist bigotry in law enforcement raised by the recent flyers will not go away any time soon. Williams, who is the only black supervisor at the West 30th Street precinct, must contend with racist attitudes in the workplace. "Some of these white officers just don't want to take orders from black supervisors," he said. "I blame the commanders at the top, white and black, who aren't saying anything about these kinds of things." And racism can also manifest itself in more than simple insubordination. A little more than a week ago, in the Riverdale section of the Bronx, off-duty transit officer Luis Baez and a friend were called "spics" and attacked by a mob of whites as they walked past the Terminal Bar on Broadway. The attack continued even after Baez had identified himself as a cop. One of the men arrested in what police are calling a bias attack was James Power, a member of the NYPD.

Three months ago, in nearby Nassau County, black correction officers filed a lawsuit in federal court against the Nassau County

Sheriff's Department. They charge that there is racial discrimination in hiring and promotion and that there is systematic harassment of black officers. One of the plaintiffs in the Nassau County suit is Correction Officer Barbara Segers, who claims to have been subjected to repeated verbal and physical harassment by white officers after she was called to testify before a grand jury investigating charges that white guards beat an inmate at the county jail. Once, about a year ago, Segers also found a dead rat on the hood of her car.

Let's hope the flyers and rat corpses are just the work of a small handful of bigots. Even so, questions remain: How many people, given the police code of silence, have failed to report these racists who should not be carrying guns and badges, who should not hold the power of life and death over others? And, if this is how rotten cops treat other cops, what hope do civilians have? . . .

NEITHER PIERRE REGIS nor New York City will forget the night of August 19, 1991, in Crown Heights. The night 7-year-old Gavin Cato was run over by a car and killed. The night Yankel Rosenbaum was stabbed to death. The night on which, some charge, Mayor Dinkins handcuffed police during a riot.

Pierre Regis remembers nothing of these urban tragedies and controversies; he only knows what happened to him.

On that summer day eighteen months ago, Pierre had just started a new job as a maintenance worker for the Heritage Nursing Home in Norwood, New Jersey. For the 32-year-old Haitian immigrant, the terror he'd left behind in 1988 – the everyday violence by gangsters in Army uniforms, the routine sadism of the ton-tons Macoutes – was quickly fading from memory. Now, the aspiring artist and part-time student at Rockland County Community College peered into the future and saw nothing but sevens.

After work on his first day, Regis visited his aunt in East New York, Brooklyn. Around 10 P.M., he said goodbye to his extended family and climbed into his red 1984 Nissan 300ZX for the drive back to

Spring Valley in Rockland County, where he shares an apartment with his parents.

The night was hot and muggy. The streets teemed with people on the loose from sweltering apartments. Regis was planning to take Flatbush Avenue to one of the Manhattan-bound bridges, when he became lost in thought somewhere in Crown Heights. He headed north on Utica Avenue and wheeled on to President Street.

He couldn't believe what he saw. Hundreds of people overflowed the sidewalks. Bottles and bricks rained down from rooftops on to scores of club-wielding, riot-helmeted police officers. A thousand Haitian nightmares flashed before Regis's eyes.

Two hours earlier, two black children had been pinned under a station wagon driven by a member of the Grand Rebbe Menachem Schneerson's caravan. The station wagon, speeding to stay close to Schneerson's Cadillac, had run a red light, hit another car, careened out of control on to the sidewalk, and plowed into the children. One of them, Gavin Cato, eventually died.

A cluster of shocked neighbors quickly turned into a wild mob and attacked the driver. The first cops on the scene ordered a Hasidic Service ambulance to spirit the driver away, moments before a city Emergency Medical Service ambulance had arrived for the children. The delay in providing medical care for the injured youngsters further provoked the crowd. By the time Regis turned on to President Street, around 10:20 P.M., police had lost control of Crown Heights. (An hour later, a young Hasidic scholar named Yankel Rosenbaum was fatally attacked by a lynch mob of blacks seeking revenge against any Jew.)

Regis panicked. He hit the gas pedal and the Nissan veered perilously close to some officers. In response, the cops rushed in front of his car. One pointed a gun at him from the passenger side. Regis put his hands up. Suddenly, the rear windshield shattered. The front windshield was battered with a billy club. Men in blue yanked Regis from the car. The last thing he remembers is an endless series of clubs and feet pummeling him as he passed out.

At Kings County Hospital, the doctor on duty when the police brought Regis in at 3 A.M. was so aghast at the young man's injuries that he called the Civilian Complaint Review Board (CCRB). Regis suffered a severe concussion and back injuries, had five broken bones in his face, had to have stitches to one eye, and lost three front teeth. He still suffers from terrible headaches and has trouble moving one of his arms.

In the past eighteen months, numerous contradictions in the police account of this beating have been uncovered by the CCRB and the district attorney's office. Investigators have now questioned seventeen cops assigned to President Street that night. All of them – including Captain William Kenney, former 71st Precinct commander – said they either weren't present when Regis was arrested or didn't see the beating. Only one highway patrolman admitted to witnessing the attack, but he insisted that he couldn't identify the cops who participated. Of those who claimed not to be present, at least six were captured on camera by the *Daily News*; they were standing over Regis while he lay sprawled on the ground.

One of those identified in the photograph, Christopher O'Sullivan, claims his left hand and right arm were injured in the rioting at 9:45 P.M. Regis was arrested more than forty minutes later. "His hand looks in pretty good shape in the photos," said a law enforcement source familiar with the probe. O'Sullivan, who has since retired on three-fourths pay, could not be reached for comment. O'Sullivan's sergeant also told investigators he was not present when Regis was beaten. But Captain Kenney claims the sergeant was at the scene, and the man is visible in one of the photographs. Meanwhile, Kenney, who has been reassigned to the Police Department License Bureau, has told investigators that he remembers ordering two officers to take Regis to the precinct, but he can't recall their names. The two cops, however, remember their instructions well and have told investigators that Kenney called them into his office later that night to review the incident.

"This guy [Regis] was badly beaten," said a source in the district attorney's office, "but he can't identify his attackers and we still have no witnesses who can."

As usual, the blue wall of silence has stood firm.

The most telling moment in that night's police radio log is the Rodney King-like admonition heard seconds after a sergeant orders his men to stop a red car.

"Careful guys," warns the anonymous cop, "they got cameras around." . . .

ONE OF THE proudest days in Ray Martinez's life was when his twin sons, Joey and John, graduated from the Police Academy in 1991. Straight out of Staten Island's Tottenville High School, where Joey had been a star baseball player and wrestler, the twins followed their older brother, Peter, on to the force. They wouldn't listen to Ray's advice and give college a try. All they could think of was serving their city in uniform, just as Peter and their father had done before them. But two years later the family has been shocked by twin tragedies and two "official stories" that make no sense.

Nineteen ninety-one was also the year that Ray retired from the Fire Department. He had served for thirty-one years, rising through the ranks to fire captain – no minor accomplishment for a Puerto Rican whose father, a cigar shop owner, had settled on 103rd Street in East Harlem in 1933. In 1960, Ray's rookie year, you could cram all the Puerto Ricans in the department onto one ladder truck. He and another young firefighter named Charlie Rivera set out to change that. They formed the department's first Hispanic Society to fight for more Latino firefighters. Charlie is now Commissioner Rivera.

With his wife, Conchita, and their two daughters, Ray moved to Staten Island's Eltingville section in 1964, where their three sons were born. Over the years, Ray worked firehouses in some of the city's worst neighborhoods and was cited three times for saving lives. By the time Captain Martinez called it quits, and he and Conchita moved to

Florida's Gulf Coast, anyone would have called the Martinez men models of devotion to this city.

Then their picture-perfect world began to crack.

In September 1992, Ray and Conchita got a call in Florida that Joey had been shot in the head while eating lunch on the job at the Staten Island ferry terminal in St George. They flew up immediately.

The doctors initially said that they didn't expect Joey to live. The bullet had passed straight through his head, from right to left. For the past six months, Joey has been in a coma. At the hospital the first night, family members said Joey's partner had told them there had been a "terrible mistake."

The "official version" that emerged within days from the Police Department was that Joey had shot himself in a small squad room with three fellow officers present. All three officers, including his partner, said they never saw him reach for his gun. Investigators have ruled out any horseplay among the cops, but they have yet to declare the shooting an attempted suicide. "We do not know why it happened; all we know is it was self-inflicted," said Assistant Chief Tosano Simonetti.

His parents refuse to believe that Joey tried to kill himself. "Joey had just called his girlfriend and arranged to pick her up after work to go and play football with his friends at South Beach," his father said. "He had everything to live for. It just doesn't make sense." Ray and Conchita moved back to Staten Island to keep vigil over their comatose son.

Then, a second tragedy.

According to Stacy, the girlfriend of Joey's twin brother John, she and the third Martinez son had argued, then reconciled, Friday morning at their apartment. They went back to bed and had been asleep for about an hour when two cops came to the door, responding to an anonymous report of a domestic dispute. Stacy assured the police that there was no problem but, as procedure requires, the cops insisted on checking the apartment. Stacy woke John. He came out of the bedroom and identified himself as a cop. An argument followed between John and the officers.

Here is where the accounts diverge. According to the police report, a third officer, James Fuginetti, arrived at the scene, hand-cuffed John, and threw him against a bedroom wall. John retaliated by biting Fuginetti in the face and trying to bite one of the other cops as well. According to Stacy, Fuginetti threw John face down on the bed and proceeded to beat him senseless with a police radio while the other cops laughed. Terrified, she telephoned John's father and his brother Peter for help. Ray could hear his son's screams over the telephone. When the fire captain arrived at the house minutes later, he found his son lying handcuffed on the bed with blood pouring from his mouth and nose and from a gash in his head. John was arrested and charged with assaulting a cop and resisting arrest. He has been suspended without pay. He, in turn, has filed a criminal complaint against the arresting officers.

This family's faith in the institutions of law enforcement has been severely tested. "I'm not bitter," Ray Martinez insisted, choking back the tears. "I just want the truth of what happened to my sons." . . .

FOR FIVE YEARS, Nina Johnson has delivered food trays to patients at Mount Sinai Medical Center. Glamorous work it isn't. But to the bedridden and helpless in strange and sterile hospital rooms, Johnson's job is essential.

When she finishes her eight-hour shift, 22-year-old Johnson hops the Lexington Avenue subway and heads for classes at Hunter College, where she is studying for a teaching degree. She supports herself on $400 a week. Johnson's co-worker, Venus Houck, raises two young children on the same salary.

The money wasn't always that good. Peter Oliver, a cook at Mount Sinai for thirty-seven years, remembers the days before the union when orderlies, maintenance staff, kitchen workers and nurses' aides made $30 a week and were treated little better than slaves. That all changed in 1959 when a small group of radical Jewish pharmacists – Leon

Davis, Eddie Kay and Moe Foner – arrived at the hospital like prophets coming down from the mountain. They persuaded Oliver and the other workers – most of them African Americans or Hispanics – to organize. A 57-day strike led by Leon Davis at the hospital gave birth to Local 1199.

During the decades that followed, Davis's union became the conscience of the city's labor movement. Although he did more to improve the lot of unskilled workers in this town than any other figure in recent memory, Davis's death in 1992 received little attention from this city's press.

Irving Selikoff died around the same time as Davis. No Mount Sinai doctor ever accomplished more for the working man. It was Selikoff's pioneering studies of construction industry workers that proved that asbestos causes lung cancer, silencing once and for all the lies of the asbestos industry. His work launched the nation's occupational health and safety movement.

John Rowe, the current president of Mount Sinai, was just a teenager when Davis and Selikoff began their fights. Like too many other hotshot executives in this country, Rowe has no idea how crucial unions were to securing workers' dignity and fortifying the workplace. A former Harvard professor who took the helm at Mount Sinai less than five years ago, Rowe now earns upwards of $800,000 a year. That's more than the president of any Ivy League college earns, more than the heads of the Red Cross, United Way and even Blue Cross are paid. In fact, Rowe is the highest-paid chief of a nonprofit corporation in the United States of America.

Let's put aside for a moment the issue of a nonprofit hospital chief making obscene amounts of money in the midst of a national health care crisis and turn our attention instead to the workers in Rowe's kitchen. A few weeks ago, kitchen supervisors told fifty workers that their hours would soon be reduced. Johnson's and Houck's hours will be slashed in half. For these women, the situation is critical. "I won't be able to afford to go to school," Johnson told me as she walked a union picket line outside the hospital.

"How can I raise my kids on two hundred dollars a week and no benefits?" Houck asked as she marched with her 2-year-old son, Christopher.

All over this country companies are cutting back from full-time to part-time workers and devising schemes to avoid paying benefits, a gutting of living standards which does not show up in the weekly unemployment reports out of Washington. At Mount Sinai, reducing the pay of fifty workers and their families to subsistence levels won't even save the hospital a half-million a year. Union leaders insist that Rowe could pay the difference out of his salary and still have $300,000 left, a suggestion that does not sit well with hospital management. "Executive compensation is not related to operations," insists hospital spokesman Mel Granick. "That's an apples and oranges situation."

Tomorrow evening, Mount Sinai will celebrate its annual black-tie Crystal Ball, where the city's elite will pay $1,000 a seat and raise more than $1 million to support the hospital's research efforts. The list of Mount Sinai's trustees reads like a who's who of New York powerbrokers – Henry Kravis, Robert Rubin, Helen Kaplan, Arthur Ochs Sulzberger, Cyrus Vance, Richard Ravitch, James Tisch, Alan Tishman, Frederick Klingenstein, to name only a few. The philanthropists will gather in the luxurious atrium of the hospital's new Guggenheim Pavilion, designed by world-famous architect I.M. Pei at a world-class price. They will hear some glowing words from Rowe about Mount Sinai's grand nonprofit mission, while they congratulate one another on what fine charitable work they do. Maybe Sulzberger's *New York Times* will even print a small society item on the ball the next day.

Meanwhile, on the very streets where their union was born, Johnson, Oliver, and Houck will join hundreds of angry Mount Sinai workers to protest the kitchen cutbacks. They will try to remind Rowe and the rich and famous at the Crystal Ball what health care is about: people taking care of people . . .

*

In 1946, JULIO MORALES left the small town of Sabana Grande, Puerto Rico to visit friends in New York City. He was twenty-one at the time and only intended to stay for the summer. So awestruck was Morales by the Big Apple that he immediately changed his plans and two months later started work as an elevator operator at the Waldorf-Astoria.

For the next forty-seven years, through recessions and wars and decades of sweeping social and technological change, Morales remained at his post, never missing a day. And, because the Waldorf is a truly legendary hotel where practically every head of state, corporate titan and movie star has stayed at least once, Morales has had an exceptional career. Not every elevator operator, after all, can boast of having transported Lyndon Johnson, Richard Nixon, Jimmy Carter, Gerald Ford, Ronald Reagan and George Bush to a presidential suite. Few can claim, as does Morales, to have personally met General Douglas MacArthur and General Norman Schwarzkopf, Frank Sinatra and Burt Reynolds, Johnny Carson and Cantinflas, Bob Hope and Dinah Shore, to name only a few. As the head elevator operator in the room service department, the trim and unassuming Morales has made it his personal mission in life to meet the needs of all VIPs, always with an infectious warmth and unflinching smile.

On August 12, 1993, at the age of sixty-eight, Morales will punch a time clock at the Waldorf for the last time. Since he announced his retirement, the testimonials have been pouring in. "If the Waldorf had a hall of fame, Julio would be up there in it," said John Fondacaro, director of front services at the 1,400-room hotel and Morales' supervisor for the last twenty years. "He's like a dinosaur, a legend here. There's few workers left like him," said Judy Knight, the young director of room service. "He goes above and beyond. I ask him to do something and he never refuses." "Always a real gentleman" is how John Doherty, the hotel's veteran executive chef, described him. "He's been my supervisor for seventeen years and I've never heard a bad word from him," said Angel Tomala. "More than a boss, he's a friend."

Morales reached early retirement age in 1987. By then, his six grown children from two marriages had produced eight grandchildren with whom he could look forward to spending his golden years. But he wasn't yet ready to leave the hotel. "I was still strong, so why retire?" he said. "I've always felt work is a responsibility you should do with pride." Now he plans to move to Los Angeles, where one of his daughters has bought a house for her mother and father. For vacations, he and his wife will visit his family's fifty-acre farm in Sabana Grande.

Julio Morales is the Puerto Rican you will never hear about on the six o'clock news. Our business is just too busy showering you with stories of welfare cheats, three-time felons, oversexed Hollywood actors and baseball stars. Not enough is said about the real heroes of our time.

2

LOS ANGELES, 1992–93

In the spring of 1992, following a Simi Valley jury's acquittal of the four police officers who had been caught on video tape beating motorist Rodney King, Los Angeles erupted in the worst riot in the US this century. The rebellion prompted then President George Bush to order a Justice Department investigation; this probe resulted in federal charges of civil rights violations against the four policemen and a second trial. I spent two weeks in LA at the time of the uprising and then returned for a month the following year, as the country waited anxiously to see whether the second verdict would throw the city into chaos again.

May 1–8, 1992

YESTERDAY AFTERNOON, National Guard troops drove down Figueroa Street and occupied this country's second-largest city. The military marched in to secure the scorched hell of South Central Los Angeles in the aftermath of the Rodney King decision, arguably the most racist verdict in memory.

A liquor store at 56th and Broadway had gone up in a flash around 1 P.M., as had its neighbor, A.J. Sedberry's Tailor Shop. "I been here twenty-five years and these motherfuckers took fifteen minutes to destroy it all," Sedberry said of the looters who had pillaged and set fire to his shop.

Sedberry supervised one young worker who was training a faint spray from a garden hose on the smoldering wall between the two stores and another who was tossing big embers from the building's roof. Inside, the shop was ruined. The interior walls were charred and most of the side wall had collapsed. Big spools of thread were strewn on the wet black soot behind the counter. Tramping through the rubble in his gray rubber boots, Sedberry appeared distressed and defeated. His shirt was misbuttoned. A blue baseball cap, emblazoned with the word Cadillac, sat askew on his salt-and-pepper hair.

"They weren't satisfied just taking the liquor," Sedberry said. "They started stealing liquor cases last night. But this afternoon I heard a big boom. I rushed out and the fire was all over the place. Koreans owned it. These kids are going after all the Korean places.

"This Rodney King thing on top of that teenage black girl killed couple of months back, that's all the excuse they needed. You know, the Korean woman who shot that girl got off with probation. Now that ain't right."

Like many of the older people in the neighborhood, Sedberry had survived the Watts riot of 1965. "I had a place over on the West Side," he recalled. "They didn't touch it. But this time . . . I may as well retire."

Just up Broadway, at 47th Street, a young black couple, Marcus and Carolyn Selestein, stood guard with their Latino kitchen staff outside their restaurant, Jacob's Cafe. Two doors away the gate to the video store came crashing down and scores of young blacks and Latinos charged in, only to emerge minutes later with armfuls of video tapes and VCRs. Parents double-parked, leaving the kids in the back seat, while they rushed in for the week's supply of movies. Five black men started shaking the gates of a shuttered variety store with a hand-written sign in the window: Black Owned Store. The Selesteins rushed over. "Now, you know your mothers and sisters need that store to shop. Don't go destroying it," Carolyn barked at the men. Like kids caught with their hands in the cookie jar, all five turned and sheepishly walked away.

"People around here figure, 'We don't own or lease any of these stores, so why worry what happens to them,'" Marcus said. "This is all just mindless kids. They don't know how long it will take to rebuild the community." He had watched last night as a crowd looted the big Broadway Food Market across the street from his restaurant. "The owner was Korean," Marcus reported. "Someone shot him in the back of the head and then people just stepped over the body as they took things out. After the cops arrived and removed the body, the people came back and burned the store."

Ronnie Harrison stood at 58th and Figueroa as a small complex of stores was engulfed in huge flames. "I was here for Watts," she said. "This is much worse. Then it was all in one area. Now, there's fires everywhere. They hit first one place, then another."

As I drove up Vermont, black smoke from more than a dozen fires spiraled into the smog. At Vermont and Martin Luther King, the smoke was so thick you couldn't see twenty feet in front of you.

"They started in Atlanta," Harrison had explained. "And I spoke to someone in Boston who said black people there are angry, too." Here in Los Angeles, though, the conflict was not solely about race. Latinos rioted, as did a few whites. More was clearly at stake than skin color . . .

*

AROUND SIX O'CLOCK on the morning of May 1st, Edward James Olmos and two friends pulled up in front of the First AME Zion Cathedral, one of the city's oldest black churches, in a garbage truck. Armed with push brooms and trash bags, they went to work in the deserted streets.

Los Angeles was just waking up from two nights of the worst looting and arson in American history. There were 38 dead, 1,300 injured and 2,000 torched buildings. The country, too, was awakening from a nightmare. In a haunting return to the 1960s, civil unrest had spread to a dozen other cities and the president had alerted troops in most major urban areas. In 1968, the assassination of Dr Martin Luther King Jr ignited rebellions in 125 cities. Now another King emerged, a man named Rodney, whose ruthless beating by crazed cops was captured on video for all the world to see. From King to King, the years of neglect, denial and economic inequality visited upon black and Latino America by the justice system and our so-called free market have resulted in a rage unleashed to frightening result.

Yesterday, a few people dared to ask, Where do we go from here? Olmos is a successful actor who grew up on the hard streets of East Los Angeles and has never lost his ties to his old neighborhood. For two days he watched his city burn to the ground at the hands of vengeful residents. "I saw whole families looting in their cars and thought of the damage this was doing to these kids," Olmos said. "I decided we had to do something. We have to get parents and their kids to rebuild this."

So Olmos got on television Thursday night and challenged the people of Los Angeles to meet him the next morning with brooms. And the people came.

He started in front of the First AME, equipped with work gloves and a push broom, and then headed south along Western Avenue through the heart of the riot area. Each block he traveled the rubble disappeared, and the cleanup crew grew. They came from the suburbs, colleges and local neighborhoods: black, white, Hispanic and Asian, young and old. All were frustrated and pained by what had happened to their city. Elias Boca Negra, fifty-one years old, brought his two sons; Tina Robinson came with her children and several neighbors' kids. "The same way it got burned down, we can get our community built up. It's called teamwork," said a young woman named Slim in a UCLA sweatshirt. "We live here. Why should we have to wake up each morning and see all this destruction?"

By noon, the group had grown to more than five hundred. They attacked the blocks of rubble energetically, filling the garbage truck with bags of charred debris. At the intersection of Slauson and Western, a parking lot overflowing with discards from the looting was cleared of trash within minutes. Clearly pleased with his group's efforts, a very grimy, sweaty Olmos offered his opinion on what should happen next: "The whole world is watching Los Angeles. We've got a generation of youth who have lost all sense of value. Maybe this will force us to do something about it." In the meantime, he added, "The politicians need to stop talking and pick up some brooms."

A few blocks away, more than a thousand people were in line at the post office. With no mail delivery, they had come for their monthly checks. The Reverend Jesse Jackson arrived and began shaking hands, kissing babies and urging people to stay calm. A young woman, Charlotte McKay, tried to talk to Jackson but broke down crying instead. "We already got the Crips and Bloods killing each other and now we got this," she wailed. "We just don't have to riot and steal and vandalize. We got to do something." Visibly shaken by her outburst, Jackson threw his arms around McKay and tried to comfort her. "He ain't even from Los Angeles but he cared enough to come here," remarked a woman in the crowd. "Where are all the other leaders, the ones from right here?"

At Western and Jefferson, about twenty-five jittery National Guardsmen, not a black face among them, were posted at a burnt-out shopping center. Across the street, Charles Jones waited for a bus and watched the guardsmen. "This is all over now. All these troops – ain't nobody going to be doing nothing. But what about the buses?" he asked anxiously. "They say most of them are running. I been waiting here two hours. I got to get downtown to get my check. There's no stores open. People ain't got food."

There are those who say the looting and vandalism have nothing to do with the verdict. These people simply don't understand. The mad violence of a group of sadistic, out-of-control cops went unpunished. This miscarriage of justice provoked even more senseless violence, this time from youths across the country who watched Rodney King being pummeled mercilessly and saw themselves on the ground. What do you expect from undereducated, alienated and unorganized youth? A rational argument? A disciplined protest? A letter to the editor? . . .

FOUR VICIOUS-LOOKING dogs snarled at me from behind the iron grates of what was once a string of shops on Vermont Avenue near 51st Street. A tall, spry, white-haired black man could be seen between the twisted pillars and steel. Protected by the dogs, 81-year-old Albert Sampson filled small buckets with water from a garden hose and tried to douse the burning embers.

Sampson, who lived in a small house behind the row of shops and kept guard over them, was overpowered last Thursday afternoon when ten carloads of looters descended on the property. "They started on the corner with the TV shop," he recalled. "Shows you how stupid they were — that was a repair shop. How did they know if the TVs they carried out were even working?" According to Sampson, the looters were of all races. A few hours later, a small group returned and set fire to the corner store.

Like many in the community, Sampson believes that the fires were too numerous and systematic to be purely spontaneous and that many were set by some of the most notorious of the city's street gangs. As if to buttress his suspicions, just a few blocks away someone had spray-painted the words "Crips, Bloods and Mexicans Together – Tonite 4/30" and "Fuck LAPD" on the wall of a burnt-out store. "I used to think that, at this age of civilization, people would know better than to do this," Sampson said, shaking his head. "I guess I was wrong."

Just then, Frank Lem, the owner of the TV shop, drove up to have a word with Sampson.

"How you doin', Al?"

"Okay, Frank. Not much left of your store."

"I know. I drove by yesterday, but my wife didn't want to stop. Thursday morning, everything was fine. Now this. At least your house is all right, isn't it?" Lem asked.

"No. All that's left is the bedroom. The fire got everything else. I got a bed, but no place to sleep in," Sampson replied.

Lem came to Los Angeles from China fifty years ago. He settled in the neighborhood, ran his corner shop for thirty-five years, raised his children here, and sent them all to the University of Southern California down the road.

"You gonna rebuild, Frank?"

"Me? How could I afford the insurance after this? No. I'm past retirement anyway. This is it for me."

At 49th and Western, Samuel and Magdalena Duarte, immigrants from Guatemala, were sitting on the stoop of a house adjacent to a giant Tru-Value Hardware Store that had been burned to a crisp. The Duartes and four other families had lived in apartments over the store until looters torched it on Thursday night. The trouble had started on Wednesday. "They broke into the store in the afternoon from the back, and all day people went in and out stealing," Duarte said. "There were police and fire trucks up and down the street all day, but they never went into the alley. That's where the stealing was."

Duarte and his neighbors stayed awake on Wednesday night, handguns by their sides for protection. "The owner is Chinese. I called him and told him to do something. He said if the police weren't doing anything, he wasn't coming down." On Thursday, the Duartes packed their suitcases and waited, still praying that no one would set a fire. Then at 10 P.M., as the couple watched coverage of the riot on

TV, Samuel heard an explosion. The floor of the apartment shook. "In no time the floor was so hot our feet were burning," he recalled. "We just had enough time to grab a suitcase, warn the neighbors, and run out." Once outside, Magdalena saw the two arsonists dash to a waiting pick-up truck and speed off. "They were Latinos. Our own people did this to us."

A few miles north, at Pico Boulevard and Hoover Avenue, the Korean owner of a photo supply store and his wife were digging through the rubble of their business. A dozen stores in the same commercial strip had burned down Thursday afternoon. "The police and firemen just stood around all day and did nothing," said the owner, J. Cho. "I couldn't believe. A hundred people robbing. They spend all day. They went from one store to another. Firemen fight big fire across street but not touch my store. Why? Why no help?"

As I drove down the streets of South Central, I fought back feelings of despair. Everywhere there were burnt-out stores, each representing the hard-fought dream of an American family; everywhere, homeless fire victims rummaging to retrieve items under a brilliant Los Angeles sun . . .

"THESE PEOPLE TRIED to loot and burn our city and we intend to make them pay for it," said Ira Reiner, the tough-talking district attorney for Los Angeles County, as he supervised the first arraignments of the more than 9,000 people arrested during the recent civil disorders. But when questioned by reporters, Reiner was forced to retract this clean, crisp sound bite. Here's what the DA forgot to mention: police failed to arrest a single major criminal during the riot.

That's right. Not one.

Despite forty-six people killed, most from gunshot wounds, a law enforcement agency has yet to charge a single defendant with murder. And despite the more than 4,500 fires that gutted whole areas of the city, leaving hundreds homeless, not one person has been charged with arson.

The bitter reality is that despite the city being occupied by thousands of National Guard and Army troops, the California Highway Patrol, federal agents, county sheriffs and police, the most vicious criminals somehow got away! The felony arrests which were made – over 3,000 in all – were primarily for burglary.

Reiner has tried to put the best spin on these outrageous statistics. Full of sound and fury, he has stated that he will "make an object lesson" of those who have been arrested. On display in Municipal Judge Glenette Blackwell's courtroom were scores of mainly young black and Latino men who had been caught carrying consumer goods out of someone's store or, in fewer cases, assaulting someone. Hauled before the judge, twenty-five at a time, the accused were quickly dispatched with a preliminary hearing date and bail set between $5,000 and $10,000.

Of course, the biggest problem with this high-speed, assembly-line justice was keeping track of which defendant was which. Dozens of public defenders, prosecutors and court interpreters shuttled back and forth from the stacks of files in front of the bench to a row of assistants seated at computers in the back who were promptly entering data on each defendant. "Who correlated these? I don't have anything correlated here," said an exasperated Judge Blackwell after she called the names of three defendants in a row only to discover that none of them were present.

The arraignments started at noon. Prosecutors were hoping to complete 600 by 10 P.M., but after only a handful a long recess was called. "The bailiff insisted that our prosecutors wear jackets and ties before the judge," shrugged Chief Deputy DA Greg Thompson. "This is Sunday. A bunch of my people came in jeans and sneakers, so I had to send them home for jackets."

In one group of twenty-five, a lone white defendant, Ian Roberts, stood. The judge set bail at $5,000. "Your Honor, Mr Roberts is buying a house in Los Angeles – I have verified that with his brother – and he is self-employed as a contractor. I request he be released on his own recognizance," said a public defender.

"Denied," replied the judge. "Next case."

Next was Tyrone Trapper, the most serious case in the group. He was charged with attempted murder, accused of trying to run someone over with a car.

"Mr Trapper, your bail is only $250,000," ordered the judge. "Next case."

As the defendants were called, DA Reiner, a one-time mayoral candidate who never met a reporter he didn't like, conducted nonstop interviews in the rear of the courtroom.

"You in the back," yelled Judge Blackwell. "This is a courtroom. Mr Reiner, you can conduct your interviews outside."

All the court employees laughed. It was one of the few light moments of the week.

As I walked out of the courthouse, I couldn't help noticing the giant plywood panels covering the entire ground floor where rioters had smashed virtually every window on the first night of disturbances. In front of the building a half-dozen Army humvees were parked, and everywhere I looked, I saw National Guardsmen . . .

AFTER THE BURIAL, everyone drove back to Jose and Henrietta Garcia's house for a bite to eat. The couple live on Siskiyou Street, a quiet, tree-lined block tucked away between the Santa Ana Freeway and Whittier Boulevard, on the edge of the old Chicano barrio in East Los Angeles. Jose and Henrietta are second-generation Mexican Americans. They grew up in this working-class neighborhood and raised their three children here.

Somehow the Garcias managed – despite four days of the rioting and a citywide curfew – to hold a wake for their 15-year-old son, Jose Luis, Jr.

The history books will record their son as just another casualty of the 1992 Los Angeles riot. This may or may not be true. What is known for certain is that around 1:35 P.M. on Thursday, near the corner of Fresno and Atlantic, a car full of young *cholos* drove past the teenager, who had played hooky from school to sneak out on his first real date. Shots were fired from the car. Jose was hit in the back and head and died within moments in front of his horrified girlfriend.

Just before the shooting, Jose had gotten into a scuffle with a gang member at Fresno Park's gymnasium and had tried to walk away. He was, by all accounts, an innocent, random victim. A tenth grader at nearby Roosevelt High School, Jose worked every Saturday in his father's mechanic shop; the gang lifestyle was no match for the garage. "He's been with me under a car since he could crawl," his father said. "Every time I turned around he and his friends had my tools spread out on the sidewalk."

In a town with some 2,000 gangs and more than 700 gang-related murders last year, his death could have very well resulted from your average deranged driveby shooting. But officials are now lumping virtually every doubtful murder committed during the last few days on to the list of riot-related fatalities. The homicide roll grows longer each day. By last night, the toll was fifty-five.

It is true that young Jose made a fatal decision when he chose to play hooky last Thursday, while other areas of the city were exploding over the King verdict. The two decisons, though, may share nothing except the calendar date. One of the barely explored mysteries of this city's descent into four days of flaming hell is how East LA – the toughest, most gang-ridden, and most infamous of the ghettos – stayed relatively calm throughout the rebellion. Other Chicano areas were also fairly orderly. In Village and Pico Gardens, the city's poorest neighborhoods with the largest concentration of public housing projects and eight active gangs, there were no fires and only a few incidents of looting.

The Reverend Greg Boyle, the Jesuit priest in Pico's Dolores Mission church, spent all day Thursday patroling his parish. "Around five P.M. I saw a bunch of neighborhood people carrying televisions and VCRs out of a warehouse a few blocks away," Boyle reported. "I stopped my car and got out. They recognized me and left immediately."

Boyle's work with gangs like Primera Flats, East Coast Cribs,

Cuatro Flats, East Side Rascals and Al Capone is legendary in Los Angeles. He employs more than forty hard-core gang members in a jobs program, has created an alternative school just for them and is building a daycare center using all "homeboy" labor. In a city overrun with homeless, Boyle provides housing for the most forgotten of the outcast – 200 undocumented male immigrants and 40 women and children who can't even get into city shelters because they have no legal identification. "Some of these men don't even have shoes. When I saw them walk in Friday with new shoes, it was a dilemma for me what to tell them," Boyle said.

Boyle believes the church's strong community ties helped prevent East Los Angeles, homebase for the older, more stable and better-organized Mexican American community, from suffering the outbreaks of violence such as those that occurred in South Central. The most violent areas in the Latino community – and Latinos were just as involved in the rioting as blacks and some whites – were the Central American immigrant neighborhoods of South Central and Pico-Union. There, gangs like the largely Salvadoran group Mara Salvatrucha were blamed by many residents for looting and fires.

"This riot wasn't about Rodney King," Boyle said. "It's about the desperation of poor people of color, about kids who cannot imagine a future for themselves. It's at such a deep, despondent level that it defies anyone's attempt to explain it rationally." . . .

THE BLACK LETTERS on the six white trucks outside Mt Zion Missionary Baptist Church spelled "Feed the Children." The shiny 40-foot rigs were parked methodically at intervals around the block, across from the green church, engines running, like settler wagons circled against the Indians.

Inside the church, President Bush was rubbing elbows at an ecumenical service with a select group of the city's elite and members of the Reverend E.V. Hill's congregation. The president's staff and the Secret Service, fearing protests by angry residents, had turned the trucks loaded with food donated for the victims of last week's riot into temporary shields, blocking sight lines for the ordinary people who had come to get a glimpse of their president. Call it food for defense.

Like everything else about Bush's short trip, originally planned as a fund-raising swing, the scene in front of the church showed just how isolated this Yale preppie is from the people he governs. "We've seen the tip of his hair," said Luis Limon. "He didn't even as much as wave." Limon, in his early twenties, was standing on a corner outside the church with his cousin Robert Ruvalcaba and about fifty neighborhood residents. "He ain't never come around here. Whenever he visits LA he goes to Century City with all his rich friends."

The first they heard of Bush's visit was when police cars began surrounding the church around dawn. The security was so tight that the Secret Service had asked television networks not to transmit live broadcasts so the local community wouldn't find out where the president was. Reporters were not given Bush's schedule of visits in advance.

Pressing the food trucks into double duty as barricades, though, testified to a new level of Republican ingenuity. The food had been brought by the Reverend Larry Jones, a Southern Baptist minister from Oklahoma City who heads a charity group called International Ministries Inc. Jones's group has been supplying food for local churches and agencies to distribute for years, and he is a personal friend of Mt Zion pastor Hill's.

"When I called and told the Bush people I was bringing the trucks, the Secret Service said, 'Fine, you've solved one of our problems,'" Jones said proudly. "As you can see, the trucks have been placed strategically by them to protect the president. Why, I even have one around back blocking access to the parking lot." Of course, with a couple of hundred reporters and cameras stationed outside the church, Jones got priceless exposure for his charity.

Inside, Bush tried his best to be relevant. "We've seen the hatred. We've got to heal and see the love," said the man who captured the White House only four short years ago by milking racist images like that of Willie Horton. But even this appeal for healing was hollow and rife with political partisanship. The neighborhood's top black official, Democratic Senator Diane Watson, for instance, wasn't even invited to the service or to Bush's meeting with black leaders afterward – although she crashed it anyway. "He has a group of leaders in there, mostly Republicans from Sacramento who do not know this area and its people" was her reaction. Neither was Gloria Molina, a Democrat and the first Hispanic to be elected to the Board of Supervisors, invited to the church service or to Bush's meeting with Hispanic leaders later in the day. Edward James Olmos, who did receive an invitation to the service because of his cleanup efforts, emerged from the church furious that Molina and other key Latino leaders had been neglected and that the riots continue to be characterized as a "black problem."

Olmos has good reason to be angry. As information about the racial and ethnic composition of those arrested for rioting is made available, the depiction of the disorders as a predominantly black uprising is being shattered. Of the first 5,438 people arrested, only 37 percent were black, while 51 percent were Hispanic and the rest were either white or of other races.

As people started filing out of Mt Zion, the Los Angeles air, which for days had been filled with the acrid smell of smoke, was suddenly filled with the suffocating aroma of heavy perfume and cologne. Politicians and ministers waited eagerly to be interviewed by reporters desperate for reactions. After a half-hour meeting with black leaders, Bush emerged from a side door. He stood on the sidewalk for several moments, talking with aides, then waved once to the crowd and disappeared into his limousine.

"It'll take more than a wave to get you reelected," yelled a white man in the crowd. His name is Robert Conrardy and he's a postal worker from Orange County. Conrardy had taken the day off with some friends to bring some food to some of South Central's homeless. "We don't need a ghost," he said. "We need someone who's going to change things for this town. I brought Bush some Carefree gum. He could use it right now."

The evidence is in. There is so much anger and frustration among the forgotten have-nots of this country and it has been building for so long that when it erupts, as it now has in Los Angeles, it becomes a sight more ghastly than any we have yet imagined. This was, after all, the riot America has always feared – the one that spilled out of the ghetto and into every corner of town.

April 4–19, 1993

THE YOUNG MAN, a gun strapped to his side and the word Security printed on the back of his blue T-shirt, stood guard outside Tom's Liquor Store. It was Friday night at Florence and Normandie. Not a soul was standing at the intersection as cars sped past. On the surface, all seemed calm.

Last April 29, the whole world watched numbly as violence erupted in this city and spread across the nation. And it was here, at this nondescript intersection in South Central, that the worst riot in recent American history began as hundreds of area residents took to the streets after the acquittal in the Rodney King case. When it was over, fifty-five people were dead; entire sections of Los Angeles burned.

Now, a year later, the fearful wait for another verdict.

"Yeah, this is where it all jumped off," said an old man in a red T-shirt who stood behind the counter at Tom's stuffing giant pickles into a big jar. "When they busted in here I told them: 'Take everything you want, just don't burn down the store.'

"But most of the ones who took stuff, they's in jail now," he added, smiling. "The TV cameras got all their pictures. They had cameras all over the place in those helicopters."

I asked whether he had seen the attack on Reginald Denny. "Nah," he replied. "I stayed in here guarding the store. But I know the guy since he was a kid. A shame, what they did to that boy." I asked if he was worried about another riot. No, he wasn't concerned: "The city's ready this time."

At Art's Chili Dogs across the street, Theodore Mitchell was closing for the night. Art's is a dinky blue-stucco joint with steel bars on its windows and only two stools for customers. Mitchell started working there after the riot. He too shrugged off the idea of a repeat eruption. "Lightning never strikes twice in the same place," he reasoned. "I love this corner. Nothing gonna happen here. You guys should be in Waco, Texas. That place is gonna explode."

In the gathering darkness, I drove down the same streets that a year ago had been sacked, gutted and engulfed in flames. To the naked eye, the extent of recovery is amazing. Whole shopping centers have been rebuilt, their garish new signs and sparkling exteriors a sharp contrast to the neighborhood's run-down houses. But there are other, sadder changes as well. On almost every block I could see smaller stores still boarded up, their owners unable to repair the fire damage of a year before.

I went back to Jacob's Cafe, a black-owned restaurant in a shopping center on Broadway near 47th Street where I had watched owners Carolyn and Marcus Selestein keep looters at bay while neighboring stores were pillaged and burned. Only their restaurant and Tam's, another black-owned diner a few doors down, were spared. Today, all the stores in the center have been rebuilt and refurbished and were open for business on the Friday of my visit. Jacob's, however, was not. "They don't open on Fridays and Saturdays anymore. Come back Sunday," said a young panhandler. "The people around here who took everything, some come around and want free food all the time. They keep saying next time they'll be back to get Jacob's and Tam's."

A few miles northwest in bustling Koreatown the fear of another riot is real and palpable. At Seoul Plaza on Vermont Avenue, two Korean businessmen were busy behind desks at the Love Cruise Travel Agency. I was barked at — "get out, get out, no time" — by one partner who was having a heated conversation on the telephone. His colleague, Chris Lin, explained the brusque evacuation order. "I live in this country twenty-five years," he told me. "Used to be Afro-Americans, Mexicans, Koreans, get along fine. No more. Now Koreans don't trust anybody, especially black. Koreans can't walk on the street here — they get attacked. Now, I buy two guns, one for my wife, one for me," Lin said, shaking his head. "All Koreans buy guns. We are ready."

Koreatown, like many of the well-to-do white neighborhoods in the city and surrounding suburbs, is filled with wild rumors of a second, even larger riot. According to local gossip, black and Latino gangs have stockpiled weapons, stolen police uniforms and targeted the suburbs for their attacks. The hysteria is so great that police have set up two hotlines for the public to monitor and counter the stories.

It is ironic, really, that this week will bring to a close one of the most important trials in American race relations. All week long, pressure and anxiety have been building around the decision and, more specifically, its aftermath. Yet, on the eve of this historic judgment, nowhere was it calmer than at Florence and Normandie . . .

JITU SADIKI, granite-hard muscles bulging under a black T-shirt, held the "hammer of justice" high in the air. It was an oversized toy made of inflatable plastic, as fraudulent and make-believe as any court proceeding in America — at least as far as Sadiki and thousands of black residents in South Central are concerned.

Georgiana Williams, a middle-aged woman in a chiffon print dress, stood next to Sadiki in a crowd of protesters outside the criminal court building yesterday. It was midday in sultry Los Angeles, and Georgiana was hot and tired. She slipped out of her worn high-heeled shoes and stood on the sidewalk in stocking feet.

Sadiki and Williams are both from South Central. A few months ago, they barely knew each other. When the riots broke out, Sadiki was in jail; Williams, a licensed practical nurse, was at work. Now they have been brought together in the aftermath of the worst civil disturbance in US history to seek the justice that racist double standards have denied them.

A long-time community worker with youth gangs, Sadiki knows

the streets as few gang counselors do. In 1975, some of his boyhood friends – members of the Bloods gang – dragged him to a party at which he fought with a member of the Crips. When the Crip came looking for revenge, Sadiki shot and killed his attacker. He was arrested and served nearly seven years in Soledad prison. While he was incarcerated, Sadiki had the rare opportunity to confront the leader of the Crips and convince him that the shooting had been a mistake. The two became close friends. Once out of jail, Sadiki dedicated himself to ending gang violence.

His troubles with the law, however, were far from over. In 1985, his brother, Danny Smith, was killed by police in a random SWAT team neighborhood search for a black man with a gun. According to police, Smith resisted putting his hands on his head while he was being questioned and, when a female officer went to move his hands, her gun misfired. The other cops, thinking she had been shot, opened fire. When the shooting was over, Danny Smith had seven bullets in his back.

Three years later, Sadiki had become a prominent neighborhood activist. His public persona did not protect him from the authorities, though, and he was arrested again, this time for attempting to rob a store; he claims police mistook him for the real robber. The officers who caught Sadiki beat him for several minutes. Later, when the cops who had seen the robber arrived and pronounced Sadiki the wrong man, it was too late. The police arrested him anyway, Sadiki insists, to cover up their beating of an innocent man. Convicted solely on the testimony of the arresting officers, he was sentenced to three years in jail in 1990. "What happened to me and my brother is what's happened to thousands of black men in this town," he said at the Equal Rights Congress, where he works. "When I heard about the rebellion in jail, I knew people had had enough."

Georgiana Williams is the mother of Damian Williams, one of the men charged with attempted murder for the brutal beating of Reginald Denny, the white truck driver whose attack, televised live by news cameras on the first night of the riots, was as horrifying to millions of

Americans as the video-taped beating of Rodney King. When Williams heard her son had been arrested in connection with the attack, she couldn't believe it. "The media said he had a long record, that he was a gang member; none of that was true." Her son, she admits, had been arrested twice for car theft while still a teenager, but he was acquitted both times and had never belonged to a gang. "I got so angry at the lies. I had to do something," Williams said. "All I ever did was go back and forth from work to church and then this happens."

Now her son faces a long list of accusations: attempted murder, aggravated mayhem and numerous other counts. Because the police who beat King were initially charged only with assault, many in the black community believe a racist double standard is at work. "In all my years, I never heard of a charge like aggravated mayhem. Is that only for black youth?" Williams asks.

Two months ago, Williams and two other mothers formed MOTHERS ROC (Mothers Reclaiming Our Children). Scores of mothers in South Central, tired of the gang violence and the stereo-typing of their children by the media, have banded together to make their presence felt in courtrooms, hearing rooms, and police precincts. They are joined in their efforts by committed activists like Sadiki, men who know first-hand the trauma caused by unequal justice. One of MOTHERS ROC's first goals is to make sure the men accused of beating Reginald Denny get a fair trial. Yesterday, while the city pre-pared for a verdict in the second Rodney King trial, the judge in the Denny case postponed their trial for three months.

For many in this city, the Denny case is as much a powder keg as the King case. "I have just as much sympathy for Denny as for Rodney King," Sadiki admits. "But black men in this country have waited long enough for equal justice." . . .

WHEN HE WENT to bed at 10 P.M. on March 2, 1991, George Holliday had no idea he was about to make the most powerful home movie ever shot. Only one other amateur effort compares to it: the Zapruder film of President Kennedy's head being blown to pieces on November 22, 1963.

But Holliday's video tape of the Rodney King beating by four white Los Angeles cops did more than just capture a horrible, tragic moment. It challenged our legal system and laid bare long-ignored racial divisions. Were it not for Holliday and his film, the Rodney King affair would have been just another invisible tale of police abuse.

The young Canadian-born and Argentine-raised immigrant, who owns a plumbing company, told me how he came to record the beating. He had gone to bed early that night because he was sponsoring one of his workers in the Los Angeles Marathon and had to be up at 5:30 A.M. to drive him to the race. Sometime after midnight, Holliday was awakened by helicopters and police sirens. He looked out of his bedroom window in suburban Lakeview Terrace and, seeing a big commotion, pulled out his new Sony camcorder, walked on to his terrace, and started taping. "I've never been in a fight in my life," said the tall, bearded redhead, "but I know I would have subdued that guy a lot sooner."

On Sunday, Holliday called the police. He was curious to learn what the black guy had done to have been beaten so badly. The police refused to comment. Then he called KTLA-TV, the local affiliate of the Tribune Broadcasting Company. They suggested he bring in the tape so they could review it. When he arrived Monday afternoon, he was told to leave the tape and the station would get back to him.

Right away, KTLA realized it had a bombshell.

A few hours later, Holliday received a call from the station requesting permission to air the tape on the 10 P.M. news. He was told that a reporter was being dispatched to interview him and that he would be paid for the use of his tape. Excited about being on television, Holliday agreed. But, according to his lawyer, Ronald Grigg, the amateur film-maker was only granting the station the right to show the tape once.

On Tuesday, Holliday called KTLA and asked for his tape back. The station offered him $500 for the right, he says, to hold on to it exclusively for a few days. At no time was he offered a written agreement. Of course, by that time KTLA had fed the tape to CNN, which had broadcast it nationally and fed it to a Phoenix station which in turn had fed it to the NBC network. Before you knew it, television stations around the world were playing the tape — again and again and again.

On Wednesday, NBC hand-delivered a $500 check to Holliday's apartment without explanation. A few days later, CNN sent a check for $150 along with a "news hound" agreement for exclusive permanent rights to the tape. Holliday refused to sign the agreement or cash the CNN check.

Before anyone had legally executed an agreement with Holliday, hundreds of stations had broadcast his amateur recording. He is now suing the networks and dozens of other stations for $100 million for copyright infringement and fraud. "This is not 'fair use' of a news event," argues Grigg. "This is corporate theft by the media!" Even film-maker Spike Lee got caught with his hand in the cookie jar when he used excerpts from the tape in his movie *Malcolm X*. He settled out of court for an undisclosed sum.

The networks say Holliday is profiteering, and that they are merely selfless public servants. Meanwhile, Holliday has set up a non-profit foundation and pledged to use all monies from litigation for programs to aid riot-torn South Central. In his private moments, he is still dogged by guilt about his video tape and the riots that followed. "Sometimes, my employees say as a joke, 'See all the trouble you caused.' In the bottom of your heart, you can't help feeling badly."

Two chance occurrences, though, have put the turmoil of the last two years in perspective. Holliday was once confronted by a cop on a city street. "You're Holliday, aren't you?" the officer said sternly, then offered his hand in friendship. "You did the right thing." Then there was the night eight months after he made the video tape when he stopped at a gas station. "Hey George, George Holliday," yelled a black man in a sporty new car that had pulled up near the pump. Holliday stared blankly at the well-dressed stranger in the car.

"You don't recognize me, do you George? You saved my life."

Suddenly, Holliday realized it was Rodney King.

"I just wanted to thank you," King said, reaching his hand out from the car window.

It was the only time he's ever met the man he made a star . . .

THE GOOD FRIDAY services were over and now the faithful poured out from St Thomas Catholic Church by the hundreds. They jammed the parking lot next to the church and the narrow sidewalks of Pico Boulevard, where a string of vendors and church associations had set up stalls to sell T-shirts with Easter messages on them, tamales, corn on the cob, sausages, rice and refried beans. The grown-ups, dressed in their best church clothes, dined under a big tent in the parking lot while their children scampered about in the warm night air. Pico-Union, the center of this city's large Salvadoran community, often seems more like a bustling town plaza in Central America than an urban ghetto in the United States.

After South Central, Pico-Union suffered the most damage during last year's riots. Virtually every store along its commercial strip was looted, mostly by a ruthless Salvadoran street gang named Mara Salvatrucha. Now, a year after the cardinal came to St Thomas to pray for peace, the terror of those days seems long gone. "There won't be any trouble this time," said an elderly man named Luis who had just attended services with his family. "You people in the media make all the trouble with your reports."

And yet, on this most sacred weekend of the Christian calendar, a jury of ordinary Americans must ponder its decision in the second King trial. What is at stake is more than just the fate of four white cops, or the possibility of yet another outbreak of violence in this and other cities. It is the potential loss of faith, for a whole segment of our nation, in the fairness of the criminal justice system.

How to explain the effect this single incident has had on the local and national psyche?

Black people look at the Rodney King tape and in every blow dealt to him feel the pain of the thousand indignities, great and small, they have had to suffer in this country for the mere fact of being born black. Some whites look at the tape and cringe at the ferocity it shows. Common sense tells them a crime was committed. But other whites, those hardened by watching too many crimes committed by blacks and Latinos, those who believe the police must be free to protect civilization from those who are destroying it, echo one of the defense attorneys, who said that the cops should have beaten King harder. Like 65-year-old veteran Joe Williamson, who plunked down $1,040 last week for a Colt .45 automatic and a Winchester shotgun, they worry that the country they live in is out of control and that politicians are powerless to restore order. So whites and Koreans buy guns, and blacks and Hispanics become more wary of the media and the cops, and everyone loses faith in the criminal justice system and our elected leaders . . .

IN THE TOWN of Compton, just south of Watts, local congressman Walter Tucker and a group of black ministers recently led two hundred black and Latino residents on a march for peace. Compton was also devastated by last year's riots. Only one business has been rebuilt. Debra Stringfield, aged thirty-five, was dropping off a friend when she noticed the crowd and decided to join the marchers who were chanting, "Let's do good in the 'hood." "Rodney King is a trial of the system," she said. "There is a lot of prejudice but rioting is not the way to deal with it. Last year we were surrounded by the fires. I don't ever want to experience something like that again."

In the days after the riots, President George Bush ordered the federal probe that led to civil rights indictments against the four cops and the current trial. Bush's actions were intended to reassure black Americans. It was as if he were saying, "Give us another chance to prove there is equal justice in this country." This week, that chance has come: the National Guard and police are mobilized, the emergency plans are ready, the gun shops are all sold out, the international media have gathered, and the vigil has begun.

If the verdict happens to be not guilty for all the cops on all the counts and the city manages somehow to stay calm, it will not matter, because the greatest damage will have already been done . . .

CRITTER WAS WORKING the cash register; Goose and Silent sat by some sacks of cornflour at the end of the 25-foot-long tortilla-making machine. They waited for Father Ted's signal to begin feeding a new day's batch of mix into the machine's stainless steel rollers. As the finished tortillas moved down the conveyor belt, two other Homeboy workers plucked them off and packed them with lightning speed, a dozen at a time, into plastic bags with the red, yellow and green Homeboy logo. At the Grand Central Market downtown, just a few blocks away from the federal courthouse where the second jury's deliberations were taking place, the Homeboys were too busy to worry about any verdict.

The workers at Homeboy come from two Boyle Heights street gangs just east of downtown – Cuatro Flats and Clarence Street 13 Cut Down. This tortilla business started after the rebellions. It was the brainchild of the Reverend Greg Boyle, the Jesuit priest who has become a local legend for his work with the youth of East Los Angeles.

In this town, gangs are more deadly than crack. One third of all the murders in Los Angeles County are gang-related. Last year, despite the much-touted truce between the Crips and the Bloods, gang killings broke the record for the fifth straight year, numbering more than 800 – nearly four times the 1985 total.

Leave it to a Jesuit to come up with something like Homeboy Industries. "Homies making tortillas? At first I thought Father Greg was just playing," said 19-year-old Critter, who never thought he could get along with a member of another gang. "Out in the street, if he's from a different gang, I don't like him, no matter what. But here we leave the gang-banging outside."

Critter was born in Mexico but raised in East Los Angeles. He's been a member of the Clarence Street clique since he was thirteen. Most of that time he was "24-7," a full-timer. I suggested it might get a bit boring just hanging out on the street all day, but Critter assured me there was plenty to do: "Every day is a new adventure. You walking down the street and get shot at, that's an adventure. Kicking in with your homies and looking for bitches, that's an adventure. Shooting up another gang, that's another adventure. Or if you're bored, you say, 'Fuck it, let's go jacking' – that's when we rob people."

Ever since Critter started working at Homeboy, however, he hasn't had much time for the gang. "By the time I get home and eat, then go over my girlfriend's and watch some movies, I'm too tired to hit the street. I got to be up early the next day for work," he explained. Critter has also managed to earn his high school diploma from the Dolores Mission alternative school. (Father Boyle convinced him to attend Dolores Mission after every other school in the neighborhood had kicked him out.) The Jesuits have a lot of faith in Critter. "He's just naturally intelligent," says the Reverend Ted Gabrielli, who now manages Homeboy Industries. "Give some of these kids a good-paying job and some direction and they can forget that life."

Goose, aged twenty, is a member of Cuatro Flats. He was born in El Salvador but also grew up here. He is a much more brooding figure than the quick-smiling Critter. "My stepfather, I never did get along with him. Instead of being a lot of problems for my mother and my family, I figured I may as well be my own problem on the street," he explained.

He left home at thirteen and has been a homey ever since. "There's no future in that life, I know that," Goose admitted. "But in a way it's fun. In another way it's dangerous. I'll always be with Cuatro Flats, always a gangster. You get respect from your friends. They watch your back. I watch theirs. They're the only family I've had." This, however, is changing. Ever since Goose started at Homeboy Industries, he's only had time to work and look after his girlfriend and new baby. "As long as I'm alive, my daughter won't want for anything," he boasted.

Waiting on the jury's decision, I drove back to South Central, past all those boarded-up storefronts. Charles Edwards stood outside his one-room Picket Bail Bonds office wearing blue suspenders, a white shirt and a tie. The front window was covered by iron bars. "I don't understand this nonsense of giving money to gang members for programs," he complained. "Did you hear how the Catholic Church gave two million dollars for gang work? I'm so sick of people making it easy for gangs."

Edwards was the first black agent for Farmer's Insurance back in the 1960s. A former president of the Watts-Willowbrook Chamber of Commerce, he believes that the government should stop coddling the gangs and should "start putting fear into people" who break the law. However, even Edwards shares the Jesuits' view that job creation is crucial to the city's future. Los Angeles's unemployment rate in February was nearly 13 percent, and the figures from South Central are much more appalling. Truth is, what this city does about the youths who gunned down 800 people last year in gang-related violence will mean a lot more to its future than the second Rodney King decision that the whole world awaits . . .

MICHAEL JAMES BRYANT's small two-chair barbershop sits on Lincoln Avenue, just a few blocks from the Rose Bowl. "Everyone around here called it the '411 barbershop,'" said Gary Moody, Bryant's boyhood friend. "This is where we came for the accurate information on everything from pork chops to baseball. Mike was the town *griot*. In African culture, the *griot* is the master informer of the tribe."

Bryant, a 6' 2", 320-pound giant of a man, inherited the place from his father. He ran it as an old-fashioned haven – a refuge really – for black men who liked to talk about the world. For stars or stevedores, the price of a haircut was the same – $10.

"Five, if you were bald," said a smiling Chuck Banks, light-bulb top hidden under a baseball cap.

Bryant's shears were not limited to local scalps. Every Thursday afternoon around 1 P.M., he would close the barbershop and head over to the NBC studios to style the heads of Branford Marsalis and cast members of the Jay Leno show. Ex-football player Mike Garrett was a regular client; so was Rick Cole, Pasadena's mayor and a former classmate of Bryant's at Blair High School. In September, Bryant would give free back-to-school haircuts for low-income kids in the neighborhood. For a while, Bryant was even Rodney King's barber.

As could be expected, Bryant soon became Pasadena's expert on the first trial of the cops accused of beating King. The town barber, though, never got a chance to follow the second trial to completion. His shop closed for good on March 9, 1993. Early that morning, barely a week into the second King trial, Bryant had a run-in with some cops in nearby San Marino. According to the official version, Bryant had hailed a police car around 1 A.M. and behaved erratically when questioned. The barber then took off in his car, knocking an officer to the ground as he fled. After a chase through three different towns, he ran into the backyard of a Highland Park apartment complex, fell into a swimming pool, and refused to come out.

Witness accounts have differed. Some have claimed Bryant was chased into the pool by cops who said, "Run, nigger, run, we're going to beat your black ass." Others say he was struggling when cops told him not to move.

The facts are that he was shot with a Taser gun, beaten with batons, hogtied, and thrown face down on to the floor of a patrol car.

Late Wednesday, as the King jury deliberated, a coroner's report ruled Bryant's death a homicide caused by "cocaine intoxication and asphyxiation from restraint procedures." An independent autopsy conducted by a group called the Friends of Michael Bryant showed that Bryant's body had twenty-six lacerations. His supporters are puzzled and angry. "He was beaten," says Moody, "and we want to know why."

Mayor Rick Cole has called on the US Civil Rights Commission to investigate the case, and Johnnie Cochran, the lawyer for the family, has filed a $20 million damage suit against the cops. Cochran also happens to represent truck driver Reginald Denny in his suit against the city. Like the Denny case this is an emotionally charged incident. Bryant was beloved in Pasadena. More than 1,500 people attended his funeral.

In any case, the fact that his tragic death occurred in the middle of the Rodney King trial has not exactly helped relations between the local black community and the cops. For years, the police in this town had a free hand under former commissioner Daryl Gates to behave as they pleased. New commissioner Willie Williams has vowed to curtail the abuse of citizens and is personally reviewing every major police abuse case. But while Williams gets his feet wet, the city is suffering from years of the cowboy mentality.

Recently, the largest civil judgment in Los Angeles history, $8.4 million, was awarded by a jury to Adelido Altamirano, a Mexican American groundskeeper at the Coliseum who was left a paraplegic by a police shooting as he was walking home from work one night. Altamirano had taken to carrying a gun for protection, since he had been mugged twice and because his walk home at night from the Coliseum took him through South Central. One evening in 1987, a mugger pulled a knife on him as he left the stadium. Altamirano fired his gun once in the air and chased the mugger away. But police who were cruising nearby heard the shot and started following Altamirano. The cops claimed that he pulled his gun on them when they ordered him to stop. Altamirano testified that the police issued no warning, that he heard a noise, turned and was hit by a bullet.

There were no witnesses and no video tape. But the trajectory of the bullet convinced the jury that Altamirano, who had never been in trouble with the law before, was telling the truth.

This week, with Bryant's barbershop closed, black men in Pasadena had no place to gather and wonder why the King jury was taking so long to decide . . .

IT WAS DARK when Davis Rodgers, still spry at the age of seventy-two, woke up to hear the Rodney King verdict. Dressed in his black cap and blue NAACP windbreaker, he walked through the Jordan Downs pro-jects, past the slate gray and blue two-story apartments, to Fred Williams's house on East 102nd Street to listen to the decision.

On the way, he passed the spot where elderly Ula Love was shot dead by cops more than thirty years ago. Love was the first of many cases Rodgers saw over the years as head of the Watts NAACP. She couldn't pay her gas bill and had protested when the gas man came to shut off the service. When police arrived, she was digging with a shovel in her front lawn to get to the gas line. She made the fatal mistake of raising the shovel in front of the officers.

In 1965, Watts burned. The neighborhood never recovered from this first rebellion. At the corner of East 103rd and Compton, next to the fire station, is a giant empty lot where thriving businesses once stood. Nearly thirty years later, the vacant lot is a haunting reminder that burning down takes minutes and rebuilding a lifetime.

Rodgers sat in Williams's cramped living room with his new boss, Ben Chavis, waiting for the decisions. When the first guilty ver-dict against Sergeant Stacey Koon was read, old Rodgers just clenched his fist and smiled a bit. Laurence Powell came next. Guilty, again. Relief swept over those assembled. Then came the not guilty verdicts against the other two officers, Theodore Briseno and Timothy Wind. Some in the room nodded in agreement.

Outside on the street, dozens of Jordan Downs residents stood in their doorways. The day was cloudy and gray.

"Those two cops were superiors, they shoulda been guilty, but the other two rookies didn't know no better," said Lee Bledsoe, who wore her hair in long braids. "They was following what the more experienced cops told them."

"I'm not worried about no verdict. It don't put no money in my pocket," said 20-year-old Tito Loc, a tall, skinny guy in a white T-shirt who said he was a construction worker. "They should've convicted all four. Only reason they got two is they thought we was going off again."

On the front steps of the house, Chavis proclaimed the verdict "partial justice." As he made sense of the verdict for those assembled,

Chavis signalled a new beginning for the NAACP, which has become almost irrelevant to poor blacks. For a generation, the organization's top leaders have been more comfortable in corporate board rooms than on urban streets. Chavis, a veteran grass-roots organizer, hopes to change that perception. More than twenty years ago he was part of the Wilmington 10. Falsely charged with burning down a liquor store during a riot in his home state of North Carolina, he spent four and a half years in jail.

As soon as he was elected, without even bothering to inspect his new Baltimore office, Chavis hopped the first plane to Los Angeles, the only place in the country a national black leader should have been yesterday. He first called his old friend Williams, who has been working with youth gangs in Watts for years, and said he wanted to stay in the projects, not in some fancy hotel downtown. For the past week, he and Williams have been walking the toughest streets in South Central and Watts, talking to gang members about strategies to stop the violence that is killing their generation.

"Nobody ever asked our opinion before about anything," Loc volunteered. "Since Doctor Chavis been here, he's talked to everybody and now people outside look at us different. We're gonna miss him."

An hour after the verdict, on the other side of the country, President Clinton interrupted a speech to praise the judicial system that brought about the verdict. Clinton said something about how the legacy of Rodney King was to "reaffirm our common humanity." As he listened to the president, Rodgers, the veteran of so many forgotten civil rights battles, began to hope for a new beginning between blacks and whites.

"This really got people talking," said Vicky Brown, who runs Victoria's Hair Salon on Normandie Avenue. "I never saw the races pulling together like this before to keep the peace and understand each other."

Nearly a year after one verdict had torn this city apart, a second began the healing . . .

*

AFTER THE RODNEY KING verdict Saturday morning, Denise Harlins left her home in South Central reluctantly and drove to the Korean American Coalition office.

After the verdict, you must understand, the movers and shakers of this town want the final image that the world gets to be that of a city recovering from a near-fatal illness. Yes, the twelve jurors in the federal Rodney King trial did what twelve other jurors in the first trial in Simi Valley had refused to do: they looked at George Holliday's home video of Rodney King's savage beating and believed their eyes. However, in this final report from the film capital of the world, I cannot offer you a happy ending.

Harlins heard the jury's verdict in her home on 91st Street and Figueroa. And were it not for that other video – the one that may have played as significant a role in last year's uprising as the King footage – she might have been celebrating yesterday. Few know better than she that a conviction is only one step toward justice, that "it ain't even a half a victory until the sentencing is done."

On March 16, 1991 – two weeks after the Rodney King beating – Harlins's niece, 15-year-old Latasha Harlins, was shot to death a block from their house by Soon Ja Du, the Korean-immigrant owner of the Empire Food Market. At first, Du and her husband claimed that Latasha had tried to rob them. But the store video camera had recorded a different story: the tape showed Latasha going into the store to buy a $1.79 bottle of orange juice, putting the bottle in her knapsack, and walking up to the counter with two dollars in her hand to pay for it. Du, fifty-one, didn't see the two dollars and immediately jumped to the conclusion that Latasha was trying to steal the juice. She jumped from behind the counter and grabbed the girl. Latasha, angered, punched her several times in the face. Du then threw a stool at the girl, who slammed the bottle of orange juice on the counter and began to walk out. At that point Du, who had been robbed several times, panicked, grabbed a gun, and shot the girl in the back of the head.

Given the video tape and Du's statement that she would do it again if circumstances were the same, a jury found the Korean woman guilty of manslaughter on November 15, 1991. She faced a maximum sentence of sixteen years. Superior Court Judge Joyce Karlin, a novice who had never handled such a big case, stunned the city by giving Du a ten-year suspended sentence. She ordered her to serve five years' probation, perform 400 hours of community service, and fined her $500.

"When I heard the sentence, I screamed, fell to my knees and cried," Denise Harlins recalled. "I just couldn't believe it. I must have died and went to hell."

A few months later, when the Simi Valley acquittals were delivered, this city had still not recovered from the Latasha Harlins case. Everyone I spoke to in the Los Angeles black community – both immediately after last year's riots and during the past two weeks – mentioned the teenager's killing and described the judge's sentence as the most unjust case they'd ever heard.

"Latasha was the heart of the people. Rodney King was just the final straw," Harlins said.

It's almost too much for a community to bear: two video-taped crimes against blacks in one year; two miscarriages of justice. Put these together with the "unsolvable" problems – the loss of 70,000 jobs, the waves of Central American immigrants who compete for low-wage jobs against unemployed black youths – and you have all the necessary firewood for the blaze that shocked the world last April.

For her part, Harlins is now leading a movement to recall Karlin from the bench and has secured a federal review of possible civil rights charges against Du. She is trying to turn the now shuttered food market into a youth center for children. Some wealthy Korean bankers have offered to help – if she will only drop the campaign against Karlin.

When she heard the new King verdict, Harlins knew that justice was still only a hope. What will prevent a federal judge from slapping the two convicted cops with light sentences? What about appeals? Saddened, Harlins went to the Korean American Coalition gathering anyway, because deep in her heart she wants the hatred to end.

3

HAPPY LAND/HONDURAS, 1990

On March 25, 1990, Julio Gonzalez, a Cuban immigrant from the Mariel boatlift who was furious with his ex-girlfriend for spurning him, set fire to the entrance of the illegal South Bronx social club where she worked. The smoke and flames trapped the patrons inside, killing eighty-seven of them almost instantly in one of the worst mass murders in US history. Most of those who perished in the Happy Land Social Club fire were Honduran immigrants. The day after the blaze I traveled to Honduras to find out who the victims were and why they had come to the US, and to chronicle their return in caskets.

When Aunt Beatrice called her name, 4-year-old Jasan Beaumont peeked out from the bedroom, her walnut eyes deep as a moonless country night. "How old are you, Jasan?" I asked. The child raised four fingers on her right hand and giggled. She snuggled up to Aunt Beatrice as the woman leafed through family albums looking for photos of Jasan's mother. Whenever Jasan spotted her mother's image she'd point to it excitedly. "She doesn't understand what's happened yet," Beatrice said. No one has told Jasan that her mom and dad are dead.

Jasan and her 1-year-old brother, Samuel Roberto, have lived in the Beaumonts' wooden house on Callejon Campo Rojo in Puerto Cortes, Honduras, with their aunt and grandmother since September. Before that, the children lived in Boston with their parents, Sam McKenzie and Daphne Beaumont. Last Saturday, Sam and Daphne decided to pay a surprise visit to Sam's sister, Hilda, and her husband, Henry Reyes, in the Bronx. The couple drove down from Boston and arrived at the Bronx apartment about 11 P.M. A few hours later, Sam, Daphne, Hilda and Henry were among the eighty-seven people killed in the closet inferno that will forever be known as the Happy Land Social Club fire.

At least ten of the victims were from Puerto Cortes.

The Beaumonts are a well-known family in this coastal town near the Guatemalan border. Dr Austin Beaumont is a popular physician, and the town numbers several Beaumonts among its professionals. Daphne Beaumont left Honduras ten years ago to study nursing in California. A few years later she moved to Boston, where she met and married Sam, the owner of a small restaurant and another native of Puerto Cortes. A few months after their son was born, Daphne decided to return to work. The couple couldn't afford daycare for two kids, so they sent Jasan and Samuel Roberto back to Honduras to live with their grandmother. Yesterday afternoon, that grandmother flew to New York to accompany her daughter's body home.

"We'll view the body right here in the house. A lot of people are coming. Daphne was very popular," her sister Beatrice explained. Of

Julio Gonzalez, the man arrested and accused of torching the Bronx club, she had only harsh words: "They should take him and burn him alive, slowly, so his skin can melt and he can feel what my sister, my brother-in-law, and all those other people went through."

As I left Puerto Cortes, I passed through the giant free trade zone near the port – factory after factory pulsing with the labor of thousands of low-paid women who manufacture clothing for American and European consumers. Miles away from the town, Jasan's innocent smile and giant brown eyes refused to fade from my mind. Nor did the image of 7-year-old Jorge and 8-year-old Pejy, the children of Sandra Beltran, another of Sunday's fire victims, who live with their grand-mother in San Pedro Sula. So many Honduran women – like other desperate Latin American immigrants, many of them illegal – are forced to leave their children behind with relatives and endure long years of separation when they head for America to escape grinding poverty.

Long before anyone ever heard of the Happy Land Social Club, immigrant suffering had already seared Honduras's heart. Out of all that misery, the corpses that return here for burial this week may be the easiest thing to comprehend . . .

I DROVE ON to Potrerillos, which sits in plantation country three hours south of Puerto Cortes. Spend a few minutes in this destitute maze of quiet dirt streets, where there are more horses, ducks and chickens than cars, where it's about eight miles to the nearest tele-phone, and you'll wonder why all the young people here have not fled to the technicolor fantasy they call *El Norte*. Many have escaped over the years and made the long journey to the United States. Six such adventurers from this town will soon return to Honduras in caskets, victims of the Happy Land fire: brothers Jose Amilcar Alfaro Paz, aged seventeen, and Calixto Alfaro Paz, twenty-two; Nicholas Zapata-Guadron, twenty-two; Lester Orlando Cruz, twenty; Wilfredo Castillo-Perdomo, twenty-two; and Jose Alexis Hernandez Diaz, nineteen.

A deep cloud of grief has enveloped Potrerillos, a town of 5,000 where everyone knows everyone else. At the dead men's homes, their mothers fashion makeshift altars in tiny living rooms. Burning candles and small, homemade crucifixes made from strips of cane stand next to photographs of the deceased along with a picture of Honduras's patron saint, the Virgin of Suyapa.

Eva Guadron, sister of the town's mayor, raised eleven children; Nicholas was her youngest boy. "He was the one I had the greatest hopes for," she said. "He was an artist . . . but how can you make money from painting here? When he left school, he went to work in the banana plantations. He'd leave for work at three A.M., toil without even eating and not return until seven at night. And do you know the most he ever brought home? Eight *lempiras*! How can anyone live on that kind of money?" After months of earning the equivalent of $2 a day on the plantation, Nicholas decided to leave with his buddies for *El Norte*. "He didn't even have a decent pair of shoes before he left," Eva recalled. "I scraped some money together and got him a pair of tennies and some new pants."

He made it to the US and found maintenance work in a New York building. Six months ago, Nicholas sent his mother a gold necklace with a medallion of Jesus Christ. "Put this around your neck," were his instructions. "If ever you are hungry, sell it to buy the food."

Early Sunday morning, Eva had a terrible nightmare. In the dream, she saw Nicholas drowning in a giant hole, flailing his arms, unable to swim. "Mommy, Mommy, help me!" he screamed. She stretched her arms out, grabbed his fingers tightly, and pulled him from the water. Nicholas brushed himself off and asked, "How do I look?" "You're beautiful, as always, my son," she answered. Suddenly, Eva's husband woke her. She was talking in her sleep. She glanced at the clock: 5:45 A.M. "Even after I awoke," she recalled, "I didn't feel right the rest of the day. I sensed something was wrong." Around 3 P.M., a neighbor brought the news: Nicholas had perished in a fire that began around 3:40 A.M. in New York.

As she recounted her dream to me, neighbors arrived with food and gifts for the family. A few minutes later, various local leaders showed up. They had come to make sure she had a ride to the airport to fetch her son's casket. "All of Honduras is dressed in black," one of the town fathers said in a soft voice . . .

By 3 P.M. ON March 29, about two hundred people had gathered at Ramon Villeda Morales Airport in San Pedro Sula to meet the plane. Airport police didn't quite know what to do with the reporters and photographers jostling to get close to the exiting passengers. The small terminal isn't used to much commotion.

This weekend, the airport will receive dozens of bodies as the Honduran victims of the Happy Land Social Club fire are flown back from New York. Honduras's new president, Rafael Callejas, has declared three days of mourning for what the country is calling its biggest peacetime disaster.

But the crowd at the airport hadn't come to mourn. They were there to get a glimpse of Yuri, a voluptuous blonde Mexican singer who is one of Latin America's biggest superstars. "There she is," screamed a small boy perched on his father's shoulders in the observation deck, a small green parrot clutching the back of his T-shirt. "Yuri, Yuri, we love you," he cried as the parrot pecked at his neck.

A hundred feet away, airport chief Pedro Aplicano was working in his small, dingy office, oblivious to the commotion. He was trying to figure out how to coordinate the arrival of the first forty-two caskets expected from the Bronx fire. Aplicano had been told a C-130 from the New York National Guard would transport the bodies. If true, it would be the second time in a year – Hurricane Hugo in Puerto Rico being the first – that Governor Cuomo had acted faster than the president in coming to the aid of people in distress.

"The plane is supposed to be here Sunday around ten A.M., but we're not sure yet," Aplicano said. "We don't have the manpower to handle the crowds that are expected. I'm waiting for the air force to tell us what personnel they'll supply." Since the country's president is expected to greet the casket-laden plane, Aplicano would like to leave security to the national government and the military, but he can't take any chances.

Jose Trinidad, a former airport security chief, remembers the time a few years back when a popular congressman from Valencia perished with his three daughters in a car accident in Mexico. "All of Valencia came to the airport to greet the bodies. We were overwhelmed." But, he added, "this could be worse. We only have sixteen policemen here."

As he spoke, Yuri's boisterous fans waited for her to emerge from customs and start her much-advertised car caravan through San Pedro. She was scheduled to give a concert that night at the town's 20,000-seat stadium, then headline a gala dance in the city's biggest hotel tomorrow. But Yuri must have taken lessons from Michael Jackson. She disappeared out a side exit of the plane, slipped into a mini-van and sped off behind music-blaring sound trucks.

"I didn't even get to see her," complained Daisy Carolina. When I asked her to comment on the appropriateness of Yuri's concert in the midst of Hondurans' national mourning, Daisy shrugged. "The people who died were our countrymen. We all feel bad," she replied. "But some mourn, others laugh. That's the way life is." . . .

IT'S ABOUT A 45-minute drive from the airport to the town square of San Pedro Sula, this country's industrial capital of half a million people. Most Hondurans who leave for America begin their journey not at the airport, as one might expect, but at this very square, which natives call Pazbarahona Park.

On a normal day, the park bustles with street vendors and crowds looking for shelter from the torrid sun. You can buy just about anything here. Friday, in broad daylight, two men examined a .38 snub-nose offered for sale, while strolling shoppers and workers looked on indifferently. Dozens of men, brazenly clutching wads of American dollars and Honduran *lempiras*, barked out black market currency rates to passers-by. The local police, M-16s strapped over their shoulders, paid no attention.

"Checks and dollars changed, right here," yelled a young man in a pink iridescent T-shirt. His name is Jorge Giovani Lopez, and he makes a good living by Honduran standards. Lopez's parents are middle-class merchants. Still, he plans to make the illegal journey soon to *El Norte*, because "no matter what you make here, there you can make a lot more."

Lopez made the trip once before, in November 1988. He and his brother-in-law Romol took the same route as many of the two hundred people who leave this city for the US every day, fleeing poverty and desperation. They first boarded a bus at 2 A.M. for a four-hour ride over treacherous mountain roads to Aguas Calientes at the Guatemalan border and then crossed into Guatemala on a five-day visa. From there, they hopped a bus to Guatemala City and then took another bus to Tecuman at the Guatemalan–Mexican border.

After Tecuman, the journey got tough. There is a small river that separates Mexico and Guatemala, and people on both sides will help you cross for a fee. "They give you inner tubes strapped to two boards of wood, and you float across," Lopez explained. "If you don't know any better, they'll charge you five *quetzales*, but the real price is one." Lopez and his brother-in-law floated as quietly as possible past the guards who patrol the river twenty-four hours a day and made it safely to Mexico. Once on land, they hopped one bus to Tapachula, a second to Arriaga, a third to Tuxtla and a fourth to Villahermosa.

In Mexico, federal police are on constant watch for illegal immigrants. "The local police, they're the first to rob you," Lopez said. "But the federal police board the buses and trains. They stopped ours and made every Latino get out. I told them we were Hondurans going to the US to work, that things in our country were bad. They let us go; but two Salvadorans and a Guatemalan – the *federales* arrested them."

The pair arrived in Mexico City near midnight on the third day and began hitching rides north with truck drivers or hopping freight trains. "We were running out of money, and we needed most of it for the *coyotes* [the people who help illegals cross the border for a fee]." It took three days to reach Tijuana.

At Tijuana, Lopez and Romol paid a *coyote* $150 apiece to lead them at night through the maze of canyons to the US border. It's a dangerous undertaking. "You've got to know how to pick the right *coyote*," Lopez advises. If not, "they'll rob you during the crossing."

Their journey to *El Norte* over, the pair walked by night up the California coast and then hitchhiked to Arizona. They were heading for Phoenix, to the home of Lopez's mother-in-law. On the twelfth day, just hours outside Phoenix, police picked up Romol. He was trying to hitch a ride while Lopez hid in the bushes. Lopez called his mother-in-law, who was also in the country illegally. She managed to get a $1,500 loan from her boss to bail out Romol. A few days later, Lopez heard that his wife was pregnant. He went home alone.

Their baby is now two years old. Lopez wants a house, a nice car. He thinks the only place he can make enough money is in *El Norte*: "I know what I'm up against. This country's too poor. People feel they have to go to America to have a future."

As he talked with me in San Pedro's bustling square, I couldn't help thinking how, in New York City, they were preparing to ship Honduran bodies home. For those Hondurans of Happy Land, the journey was over . . .

JUST AFTER 9 A.M. on April 1, the jumbo jet cargo plane arrived at Ramon Villeda Morales Airport carrying the caskets of forty-eight of the Hondurans who died in the Happy Land inferno. As the red-and-gold-striped plane taxied to a halt, it released first a deafening roar and then a screeching wail that sounded almost human. The plane's cry echoed over the four hundred relatives, soldiers and reporters waiting outside the terminal and was met by anguished screams from the crowd. Everywhere you turned, relatives were starting to faint in the sweltering heat. Honduran soldiers and Red Cross volunteers tried desperately to keep order while treating those overcome by grief.

Inside the terminal, President Rafael Callejas and his wife, Norma, several generals and the Catholic bishop of San Pedro Sula waited in the air-conditioned VIP lounge for the caskets to be unloaded.

It took more than an hour to arrange the boxes in neat rows in front of the grieving relatives. Suddenly, the crowd surged forward as relatives scampered to find the caskets of their loved ones, and pandemonium ensued. More people collapsed, either on to the ground or on to the caskets.

Then Callejas and Monsignor Jaime Brufeau stepped outside the terminal. The bishop said a few prayers, threw some holy water on each casket, and hurried back inside. The president, barely two months in office, spoke to the press from behind dark sunglasses and followed the bishop inside. Not once did either the bishop or the president offer a word of condolence directly to the assembled relatives or touch the hand of a grieving mother. "What lack of respect for us," said one disgusted mourner who had traveled eight hours from distant Colon.

Around 11 A.M., residents of Potrerillos loaded six caskets on to pick-up trucks. More than a hundred people from the small town jammed on to other pickups and cars, and the caravan took off. I was one of them. As we neared the town, hundreds were standing along the highway to watch the procession. We turned on to the dirt-and-rock main street that leads to the town square. The church bell rang and a siren sounded from the lone town ambulance. The procession passed once around the small square before each family took its casket home . . .

SAN PEDRO SULA'S cemetery, Jardines de Recuerdos, sits on a few of the rolling hills which ring this town like an emerald necklace. On April 2, they buried 17-year-old Yanet Castro in one of those lush green hills. Two hundred yards away, Osvaldo Cruz was laid to rest. Later, Sandra Beltran. It was my last day in Honduras.

As six cemetery workers lowered the concrete slab into the grave over Yanet's casket, her mother, Marta, dressed in a simple black dress, began walking, head bowed, toward the parking lot. Yanet's father, Julio Castro, immaculate in a blue sports jacket, white pants, and a black tie emblazoned with the Playboy logo, sat by the grave, cradling 2-year-old Carlos Roberto, his dead daughter's son, in his arms. He has cared for the boy since Yanet left for the United States shortly after the baby's birth. Yanet's mother and father have not spoken in years, since their separation when Julio won legal custody of their three daughters. Even during the funeral they avoided each other, in a grim sideshow.

While I had witnessed many poignant incidents in San Pedro Sula, none equaled the Cama Nacional Funeral Home on Sunday night, where hundreds of local residents had filed by Yanet Castro's casket and those of nine other Happy Land victims. I went with David Handschuh, the *Daily News* photographer who traveled with me to document these sad proceedings. David was snapping photos in the funeral home when he suddenly recognized a fellow he'd known in the Bronx. Felipe Menaiza had been the night doorman in the Riverdale highrise where Handschuh had lived before marrying and moving to New Jersey a year and a half ago. Over the years, Menaiza and Handschuh had become good friends, but they had lost touch after Dave moved out.

"What are you doing here, Phil?" Dave asked.

"Four of the kids who died in the fire were mine, Dave," Felipe said calmly.

In the middle of the funeral home, the stunned photographer put down his camera and embraced his former doorman.

March 28–April 3, 1990

4

THE MURDER OF MANUEL DE DIOS UNANUE

On March 11, 1992, Manuel de Dios Unanue, a veteran Spanish-language journalist and editor, was assassinated in a restaurant in the Jackson Heights section of Queens. De Dios's mysterious murder touched off a massive federal and local investigation. The *Daily News* and other New York-based media institutions offered more than $60,000 in reward for information which would lead to the arrest of the assassins. Six Colombian immigrants were eventually arrested and convicted of planning and executing the killing. They were working on orders from the Cali cartel, hired to silence the journalist from exposing the organization's local operations. To ensure that de Dios's work would not be forgotten, a handful of us in the English-language press stepped up efforts to report on the police investigation of his death and to publicize the workings of the cartel. I say a handful because his death made clear to me how blind and dismissive my colleagues in the mainstream press are toward the world of foreign-language journalism in America and revealed the unexamined racism which pervades even this most probing of professions.

ON THE NIGHT of March 11, 1992, just minutes after speaking by phone with his wife and 2-year-old daughter, Manuel de Dios Unanue returned to the bar of Meson Asturias, an upscale restaurant in Jackson Heights. According to police, he sat alone with his back to the door. At 9:15 P.M., he was shot twice at point-blank range in the back of the head.

"It doesn't make sense," said long-time friend Gerson Borrero. "He never ate alone, and he certainly never sat with his back to a restaurant door." Caution had become habitual to de Dios, a journalist who had survived years of death threats including a botched attempt to firebomb his office. In truth, de Dios was as fearless a reporter as this city has ever seen. Those of us who knew him and marveled at the risks he took, worried that one day he might die this way. Manuel had made countless enemies in his almost messianic pursuit of what he regarded as the truth.

Manuel had always lived fearlessly. He fled Cuba for Puerto Rico in the early 1960s. There he earned a degree in criminology from the University of Puerto Rico and became a protégé of Senator Marcos Rigau. In 1973, Rigau got him a job in New York with the Commonwealth of Puerto Rico, and he later began work as a reporter for *El Diario-La Prensa*. Although an opponent of Castro, Manuel committed the cardinal sin for die-hard anti-Castro Cubans when he visited his homeland and interviewed Castro in the 1970s. In his published reports from Cuba, Manuel even expressed grudging admiration for the Cuban leader. Soon after the trip, his newspaper was firebombed by an anti-Castro underground group.

In the early 1980s, Manuel became an expert on the growth of the Colombian drug cartels. When the Gannett chain, which briefly owned *El Diario*, refused to cover the trial of Medellin cartel leader Carlos Lehder in Florida, Manuel paid a reporter out of his own pocket to cover the courtroom proceeding. Later, he wrote a book, *The Secrets of the Medellin Cartel*. It was a strange work. While detailing the operation of the cartel, the book also seemed to almost praise drug-dealing Lehder's anti-American ideology.

The journalist's stand against drugs, though, was never in question. For several years he had a daily radio talk show on WADO-AM called "What Others Try to Silence." In an unprecedented move, he began broadcasting the names of drug dealers operating in different neighborhoods of the city. Listeners would phone in tips to Manuel off the air. He would then notify the police before releasing the names of suspected dealers to his radio audience. Manuel seemed almost to dare dealers to retaliate. He could always be found walking, alone and unprotected, on the streets of Jackson Heights and other Latino neighborhoods. Over lunch, he once offered to introduce me to some people he believed were among the top leaders of the Cali cartel operation in New York.

Manuel resigned from *El Diario* a few years ago after a falling out with the publisher and soon after began publishing a magazine. Recently, he started a new journal, *Crimen* (crime), and just last week, in the first issue, published a scathing article about money laundering by drug rings in Queens. He named names. "He never compromised in what he believed, and he had a habit of going after people in public in a way that made them furious," remarked one of his close friends . . .

THE POLICE OPENED their investigation into the murder of Manuel de Dios Unanue on March 12, 1992, complaining about the list of suspects that's as long as a phone book. The most logical place to start, however, is with the lead that de Dios himself was doggedly following just before his death: the Cerro Maravilla murder case. The trail of questions should begin not in Queens but on a Puerto Rican mountaintop.

On July 25, 1978, two young independence advocates were lured by an undercover informant to participate in a planned bombing of a television station tower on a mountaintop called Cerro Maravilla. When the pair arrived at the meeting point twenty officers were waiting in ambush. The police later claimed there had been a shoot-out in which the two young men were killed. A few brave Puerto Rican journalists, unconvinced by the official explanations, relentlessly pursued their own investigations.

Several years later, a Puerto Rican Senate committee convened to consider the case. Their investigation revealed that the young men had been murdered in cold blood while pleading for their lives. The first hearings put ten former cops on the island in jail for perjury, two for murder. The committee also found that all of the officers involved had conspired to cover it up. It was Puerto Rico's Watergate, a political drama that garnered the highest television ratings ever on the island. The case was even the subject of two books and a Hollywood movie.

The hearings on Cerro Maravilla were recently reconvened by the Judiciary Committee of the Puerto Rican Senate. Many people on the island were unsatisfied with the outcome of the first hearings and still suspect that the conspiracy extended to the top levels of the Puerto Rican government, possibly to former governor Carlos Romero Barcelo, perhaps all the way to Washington.

On February 25, two weeks before his death, de Dios was called to testify before the Judiciary Committee. On the stand, he did something unheard of for a reporter: he revealed a confidential source for an article written one month before the 1978 murders. His article had quoted an unnamed Puerto Rican intelligence official who predicted an upcoming wave of violence on the island. That official, de Dios testified, was retired colonel Desiderio Cartagena, once the second-highest ranking police official on the island. When Cartagena appeared before the committee, he denied even knowing de Dios. But de Dios presented photographs of the two of them together.

Top Puerto Rican government officials now say that de Dios's testimony guarantees that Cartagena will be indicted for perjury. Yesterday, before the journalist's body had even been embalmed, Cartagena finally admitted to the Senate committee that he had lied about his relationship with de Dios and, in fact, about other matters concerning Cerro Maravilla.

But the scandal doesn't stop there. After years of refusing to release its files on the case, the FBI is now cooperating with the Puerto Rican Senate. During the past few months, the committee has heard chilling testimony about right-wing death squads composed of Puerto Rican policemen, former FBI agents and US Army officers. Death squad operations on the island in the 1970s involved the fabrication of terrorist attacks to blame on the Puerto Rican independence movement and planned assaults on the movement's supporters.

When he returned from Puerto Rico for the last time, de Dios told friends that he had uncovered new information linking anti-Castro Cubans, the death squads, and drug traffickers. He thought he had material for a new book and was seeking financial support while he unearthed the full story. He never had the chance . . .

ON MARCH 14, de Dios was buried in Hato Rey, Puerto Rico. The casket was closed, in accordance with his instructions. Years of death threats had forced him to think about his own funeral. "I don't want my killer or any hypocrites to laugh at me in a box," he had told close friends. Manuel de Dios was buried the way he had lived – frustrating his enemies and taking with him the secret of yet another conspiracy, that of his own killers.

About 150 people filled the chapel of the Buxedo Funeral Home to pay their last respects to the Cuban-born writer and editor. The crowd was small according to the family's wish for a private burial. His younger brother Jose, a taller version of Manuel, organized the funeral. Seated next to the casket were de Dios's mother, Teresa, the sisters and brothers who owed him their lives, his second wife, Vicky, and his 2-year-old daughter, Melody. The toddler fidgeted in Vicky's lap. Each time her small stuffed dog tumbled to the floor, Melody shrieked in delight, her voice echoing above the priest's. She was de Dios's only child, a late addition to the life of the 48-year-old crusading journalist.

De Dios was laid to rest in Puerto Rico, in his adopted land, where his mother and two of his sisters reside. This refugee from

Cuba won his family their freedom as well. He interceded with Cuban authorities until they agreed to release his younger brother, a die-hard anti-Castro militant, from a political prison in 1978. Over the years, de Dios succeeded in bringing all of his brothers and sisters out of Cuba. But his efforts came at a price. He had to negotiate with the Cuban government, something the more radical right-wing Cuban exile groups vehemently condemned. These are the same extremist Cuban groups whose ties to Puerto Rican death squads in the Cerro Maravilla case de Dios was investigating just before his death.

"The one who did this is a very important person," de Dios's brother said yesterday of the murderer. "That person, I am sure, is completely scared." His brother does not know if Manuel had given new information to law enforcement groups before his death.

"More than a victim, he's a hero," said Senator Marcos Rigau, long-time friend and mentor of de Dios, in a tearful eulogy at Los Cipreses Cemetery in Bayamon. "A Cuban hero. A Puerto Rican hero. Through Manuel, I learned to love Cuba."

Family members placed on the casket two copies of *Cambios 21* and *Crimen*, the magazines de Dios was editing before he died. Colombian-born Vicky has vowed to return to Queens to keep publishing them. When the casket was lowered into the ground, little Melody could be seen curled up in a chair. Her mother, swollen eyes hidden behind dark sunglasses, sat beside her, clutching the small stuffed dog . . .

A YOUNG DRUG "mule" arrested by federal customs agents at Kennedy Airport in late March claims he witnessed the payoff of Manuel de Dios Unanue's killer in Cali, Colombia, by the major drug dealer responsible for the assassination. The young man will not speak to New York City homicide detectives or testify in court without a guarantee of immunity; federal authorities are now deciding whether or not to offer a deal. "This guy might be a nut case, but this really should be explored," said one law enforcement source.

Rafael Perez, who was arrested on March 25 when he tried to smuggle a pound of heroin into the country on a flight from Cali, looks younger than the fifteen years listed in his Colombian passport. He is actually in his early twenties. Perez claims that a few days before leaving for New York with his assigned heroin shipment, he was present at a meeting in a Cali office building when the payoff for the de Dios slaying was made. He says his boss – a major figure in the Cali cartel – paid $20,000 to a tall, dark-skinned Colombian assassin who had just returned from New York after completing his mission to kill "the journalist."

This suspect now puts law enforcement authorities in a quandary. More than a month has passed since the cold-blooded execution, yet police admit they still have only suspicions, no concrete leads. His story dovetails with police suspicions that the de Dios killing was ordered by a cartel member in Colombia, where more than fifty journalists, hundreds of police and a fair number of judges have been executed. But questions remain: Is Perez just a scared kid trying to con his way out of a jail term? Or is he the key the police have been waiting for to unlock this baffling case?

This is what is known: Perez arrived in this country three years ago and found work in a factory in Elizabeth, New Jersey. Last September, a major Cali dealer whom he knew from the streets of Elizabeth offered him $2,500 up front and $13,000 on delivery to smuggle a pound of heroin into the US. Perez jumped at the chance to make some real money. He flew to Cali immediately and spent a few months with his family until his boss, who by that time had returned to his local office, called Perez to pick up his plane ticket and the drugs. When Perez visited the office to collect his assignment, he claims that he witnessed the arrival of the assassin and the payoff. For the first two weeks after his seizure by customs, Perez kept quiet. Then he learned that his boss had ordered the shooting of his 16-year-old sister under the assumption that Perez had fled with the shipment. The girl survived the shooting, but it turned Perez against his boss. According to sources, Perez is now willing to identify and testify against him. In return, he wants only to be guaranteed protection by the federal government. Perez knows he will probably spend some time in jail. His lawyer, however, aware of the value of his story, is pressing for complete immunity.

For their part, law enforcement sources question whether Perez is mentally stable. While they ponder their next move, many people in this town are growing impatient with the lack of progress in the investigation . . .

ON NOVEMBER 4, 1993, after fourteen months of relentless work by federal and local investigators, the first glimmers of truth began to emerge in the de Dios murder case. Most important of those truths: De Dios was killed because he was a journalist, because he wrote about the international underworld of drugs, and because Jose Santacruz Londono, one of the chiefs of Colombia's Cali cartel, wanted him silenced.

This was made clear by the first federal indictments of 18-year-old Alejandro Wilson Mejia Velez, the assassin, and John Mena, the small-time Queens drug dealer who paid him according to Santacruz's instructions. A half-dozen other Cali operatives are now in custody and more indictments are expected. While they wait in jail, their boss – the Colombian druglord who ordered the assassination of an American journalist on US soil – remains a free man because Colombia and the United States no longer have an extradition treaty.

For a while, a few supposed journalists chased wild rumors that the always controversial de Dios was killed for bad debts, or for having shaken down businessmen in Queens, or for some other personal reason having nothing to do with his reporting. The indictments lay to rest all that vile speculation.

They also serve as a clear indication that drug cartel terrorism has broken out of the narcotics underworld and into the American newsroom. Even before de Dios was murdered, many reporters in the semi-obscurity of the Spanish-language press refused to cover a drug story or to put their byline on articles about the drug trade for fear of retaliation. I have been warned by police officials on several occasions to stop writing about drug traffickers if I want to stay alive. I have even received threats for following the trail of de Dios's murderers. While Latin American reporters have suffered from this kind of gunpoint censorship for years, few expected it would reach all the way to the birthplace of the First Amendment.

According to investigators, all it took to kill de Dios was a $1,500 payoff to a crazed teenager and a few thousand more to his backups and handlers. That is how cheaply the life of a journalist can be had in the drug world. But, of course, it's not just journalists whose lives are threatened. In Queens, thousands of hardworking Colombians live in daily fear that anything they say about the Cali or Medellin traffickers could bring violent retribution. They are keenly aware that scores of unemployed *sicarios* (assassins) are now in the United States, hiding out from Colombia's crackdown on the cartels . . .

JOHN HAROLD MENA took the witness stand in a Brooklyn federal courtroom on February 23, 1994. In the first row of the courtroom sat Teresa de Dios, dabbing away tears with a wet handkerchief and repeatedly stifling sobs as she listened to Mena testify about how he and a group of cold-blooded killers from a branch of the Cali drug cartel planned and carried out the murder of her brother. In this city of endless murders, the March 11, 1992, slaying of de Dios was unique in New York history. According to police, de Dios was killed not for money, or love, or revenge, but for words.

"He was publishing a lot of things about the people of Cali," Mena testified. The 25-year-old once managed the New York business for one of the main Cali drug families, the branch run by Jose Santacruz Londono, also known as Don Chepe. As a key Don Chepe operative, Mena distributed more than 3,000 kilos of cocaine and participated in three murders in Florida and Maryland before de Dios's number came up. He claims to have been told by his brother-in-law,

Guillermo Leon Restrepo, that there was a $50,000 contract on de Dios's head. "He was going to publish a book [about Cali] and Don Chepe didn't like it," he offered by way of explanation.

Drug traffickers from Cali, unlike the now-decimated Medellin cartel, dislike publicity. They are a low-profile, business-only group. Because of that, few journalists in this town can even name the major Cali families. When de Dios decided to write a book on the Cali cartel, as he had years before on the Medellin, he was marked for death. Is there a greater tribute to a journalist than to label him too dangerous to live?

5

FREE TRADE: MEXICO AND THE CARIBBEAN, 1989–95

Wall Street calls it free trade. For Latin America, it arrived first in Puerto Rico in the 1950s with a tax-exempt industrialization program called Operation Bootstrap; it then spread to the US–Mexico border in the 1960s and 1970s with the establishment of American-owned factories or *maquiladoras*; to the whole Caribbean rim in the 1980s with Ronald Reagan's Caribbean Basin Initiative; and finally to all of Mexico in the 1990s with the North American Free Trade Agreement. Everywhere "free trade" has meant super-cheap labor, freedom from import duties and minimal labor and environmental controls for US companies willing to desert American cities and American workers. But the cost to host countries, and especially to workers in these zones, has been incalculable. To visit any of the free trade zones and the shantytowns that have sprung up around them is tantamount to returning to the Dickensian days of early capitalist England.

NEW YORK, NEW YORK — One morning in October 1988, Ana Garcia and 450 other women filed through the factory's gates in Zone 14 of Guatemala City to start another week of stitching clothes for America's closets at thirty cents an hour. Instead, they found the plant locked, the sewing machines ripped out and their bosses gone — no warning, no note, no final paychecks. Where only days before 300 machines had been mounted on platforms, now only motors, ripped wires, empty pushcarts and giant industrial washing machines remained. Oh yes, and the piece of paper tacked to the wall.

In their hurry to cram the machines into trucks and speed away before sunrise on Monday, factory managers had left behind a sheet of phone numbers for a half-dozen of their other plants in countries such as the Philippines, Hong Kong and Sri Lanka. At the top of the list, in Spanish, were the words "main office" and the phone number for Play Knits, Inc., a Manhattan-based outfit.

Three months later, Garcia and about one hundred of her ex-coworkers are sitting in the empty factory in Guatemala; they have been occupying the building since that October morning. Nearly twenty of the women are pregnant. For some, the big factory is now their permanent residence since they were evicted from their homes when they could no longer pay rent. All are hoping that the Guatemalan government — or someone — will force the runaway owners to obey Guatemalan law and pay not only severance but also their last week's wages. But, in the world of multinational companies, what it means to obey the law is not straightforward.

Nowadays, so much of our nation's wealth is stripmined, at dirt pay, from muscle and sweat inside the factories and mines of Asia, Africa and Latin America that our eyes will never discern the terrain of ravaged bodies, nor inspect simulations on computer terminals. But just because we can't see it, or just because it's legal, doesn't make it right for American companies to treat human beings in foreign countries in ways we would never tolerate here.

Last Friday, a group of local union leaders went to the offices of Play Knits, Inc. on West 40th Street to say just this. Led by Sandra

Bermejo, the secretary-treasurer of the Joint Board of Headwear & Allied Workers in New York, the delegation hoped to meet with Ralph and Saul Tawill, the president and secretary of Play Knits respectively. Both are listed, according to union leaders, as officers of Confecciones Transcontinentales, the Guatemalan plant that closed suddenly on October 4th.

Before closing, the plant had manufactured clothing for the Liz Claiborne and Willi Smith sportswear lines for two years. At one point it employed 1,700 workers. Last summer, the employees decided to unionize after a series of massive lay-offs. They took the company to court in Guatemala for unfair labor practices and won legal backing. According to Ana Garcia, the company responded in early September by removing some equipment and declaring work holidays. A few weeks later, the plant closed.

Now the workers are in court again, trying to get the money owed to them, but they can't find either the former plant manager or any of the owners. Meanwhile, they've effectively seized whatever equipment is left with their sit-in.

Last Friday, after being informed that the Tawills were away on vacation, I managed to speak with the company lawyer, Jeffrey Pagano. To his mind, the Guatemalan company is a "separate and distinct operation." "As far as I can see, there is no dispute with Play Knits in the US. If there is a dispute," he added, "it must be resolved in Guatemala, under Guatemalan law." I told him about the paper on the factory wall, the one that listed Play Knits as the main office, and asked whether the Tawills were indeed officers of the Guatemalan company. "Let's assume those facts are true," he replied. "They [the workers] can't legally go after the parent [company]."

Earlier, Ana Garcia had told me on the phone about how hard it is to find a job in Guatemala, even one paying what amounts to thirty cents an hour. I thought of the 450 breadwinners out of work, of Garcia and her one hundred coworkers spending three months in an abandoned factory with no electricity in a desperate attempt to salvage a little dignity and the few miserable dollars owed to them by a company based thousands of miles away. And here was this smart New York lawyer telling me about "separate and distinct" operations while his clients were on vacation. If the Tawills are lucky, they may even find another Third World country where you can pay people less than thirty cents an hour to fill American closets. Then those sewing machines will find a new home and new hands. (January 10, 1989)

NEW YORK, NEW YORK — From a pay phone at the Red Parrot Inn outside Roanoke, Virginia, Jose Luis Delgadillo called me to apologize. He would not be on time for our meeting; although he had left the Mexican border town of Matamoros early Monday morning as planned, the drive to New York was taking longer than expected. "No matter," he said. "I'll be in front of the United Nations tomorrow with some of my neighbors. We want the world to know Salinas doesn't deserve this award."

Today, on World Environment Day at the United Nations, Mexico's president, Carlos Salinas, will be honored with the first-ever Earth Prize. Most people would argue that for Delgadillo, a dollar-an-hour Mexican mechanic, and some friends to travel 2,000 miles in a rental car just to protest a ceremony New Yorkers will barely notice seems a bit odd. Delgadillo's action, however, is less bizarre than the one that provoked it.

And stranger still is the awarding of a prize to the Mexican president for anything. After all, Salinas was elected a few years ago in a contest so corrupt that it made Manuel Noriega's electoral activities seem squeaky clean in comparison. While in office, he has received international praise for setting up a 2.5 million-acre sea reserve as a breeding ground for the gray whale and for his program to save rare species of turtle. Less publicized was his decree in January establishing a mile-and-a-quarter "protective zone" around a major chemical plant in Matamoros, a sprawling city with a population of 400,000 across the Rio Grande from Brownsville, Texas. The decree calls for the government to remove 30,000 residents of the zone to prevent a possible catastrophe in the event of a gas leak. Salinas, the Earth Prize honoree, has proven that he cares more about protecting the habitats of gray whales and marine turtles and the investments of his rich friends than the homes and lives of his less well-off constituents.

The Matamoros plant, Quimica Fluor, was built in 1975. It is one-third owned by Dupont and two-thirds owned by a group of Mexican investors headed by one of Salinas's best friends, magnate Carlos Slims. Quimica Fluor produces hydrogen fluoride (HF) which is used in oil refining. Every time you pick higher-octane gas at the pump, you're paying extra money for the hydrogen fluoride they spiked it with back at the refinery.

Liquid HF happens to be one of the deadliest chemicals around, capable of Bhopal-like destruction. According to recent studies, an accidental spill of only 1,000 gallons has the power to kill all human and plant life within a 5-mile radius and to cause severe skin burns, eye and lung problems to individuals as far away as 7½ miles. As Dr Fred Millar, a specialist in toxic chemicals with the Environmental Policy Institute, explains, "When released, HF forms a dense cloud which hugs the ground and rolls with the wind in an ever-widening 'plume.'" During testimony before the California legislature in 1988, Millar detailed the history of HF spills in this country and argued that the chemical industry has often kept quiet the results of its own research on the dangers of the gas.

After the Bhopal disaster of 1984, in which over 2,000 people were killed, the threat posed to local communities by chemical companies and their products was finally recognized and stringent restrictions were enacted in leading industrial nations. Companies have increasingly chosen to relocate to Third World countries to take advantage of weak environmental laws and lax regulations. Of course, they are hardly beating a new path: on the Mexican border alone, there are more than 2,000 mostly American-owned factories employing a half-million workers. The average pay in these factories — known as *maquiladoras* — is eighty-eight cents an hour.

Matamoros has seen its share of *maquiladoras* of the chemical stripe. "There are four other chemical plants in this neighborhood beside Quimica Fluor," said Maria Teresa Mendez, who has lived in the town for thirty years, since long before the plants were built. "I've been evacuated from my home three times because of leaks. The last time was in 1990, when there was one at Retzlos."

Realizing that any leak at Quimica Fluor would result in a human and political disaster of epic proportions, Salinas had only two choices: move the plant or move 30,000 people. He chose to move the people.

"We fully support the president's decree," said Quimica Fluor director Alfonso Ruiz Fernandez. "The cost of moving it [the plant] would be such that it would be the death of the business.

"Obviously, there has been some uneasiness on the part of the residents," he said of recent mass protests in the town. "I can understand that."

One can only hope Fernandez understands why Jose Luis Delgadillo and a few poor neighbors jumped into a rental car and drove 2,000 miles just to let the UN know about its mistake. (June 5, 1991)

SAN PEDRO DE MACORIS, Dominican Republic — Tetelo Vargas Stadium is the closest thing San Pedro de Macoris has to a shrine. It is where most of the great Dominican baseball players first displayed their skills to hungry US scouts. George Bell, Pedro Guerrero, Julio Franco, and Juan Samuel were all raised on the sandlots of this coastal city, fifty miles east of Santo Domingo.

But although the outside world knows San Pedro only for its homegrown athlete-millionaires, a few blocks from the stadium, on hundreds of acres enclosed by wire fences and guarded by armed police and soldiers, lies the town's real source of manufactured wealth: La Zona Franca. This vast free trade zone brims with ninety factories manned by 40,000 employees, primarily young men and women who labor in sweatshop conditions reminiscent of late-nineteenth-century Manhattan.

Mayra Jimenez was fourteen when she started working at Tejido Internacional, a garment factory. She then moved to Camisas Dominicanas, which manufactures polo shirts. At age nineteen, Mayra lives in a tiny house in Barrio Restauracion, a tough, sprawling ghetto of wooden shanties, dirt streets and outhouses not far from the Zona Franca. I spoke with her about working conditions in the zone. "Every so often the factory manager would tell those of us who were under-age not to come in the next day," she recalled. "He'd been tipped off that a government inspector would soon come around looking for children, and he wanted us out of the way." Mayra, who is smart and articulate, said she couldn't bear the daily mistreatment: working twelve- to fourteen-hour shifts and then getting cheated out of full wages, being forced to eat lunch on the factory floor, having no clean drinking water and sharing one toilet with one hundred coworkers. And she told me of other injustices as well: workers are routinely injured on the job but there is not one ambulance in the zone to transport them to hospital; employees at one plant have suffered severe lead poisoning from unsafe soldering practices; sexual harass-ment is so widespread that lists of women fired for resisting advances have been brought to the attention of the Dominican Congress.

When she was eighteen, Mayra organized a one-day strike for a union at Camisas Dominicanas. Three weeks later, she was fired and her name was circulated on the owners' association monthly blacklist of workers in the zone booted for troublemaking. Since the law here does not protect workers who are fired for union activity, Mayra can no longer find work. As for unemployment insurance or welfare, neither exists in the Domincan Republic.

These facts have not deterred her or Luis Mojica, the soft-spo-ken leader of the Federation of Provincial Workers of San Pedro de Macoris, from continuing their fight. In just a few years, Mojica has succeeded in organizing unions at twenty-three of the ninety factories. On July 9 and 10, leaders of the CTU, a national labor federation, organized a general strike to protest runaway inflation, which last year alone was 106 percent. Although only 15 percent of the country's labor force is unionized, 90 percent of Dominican workers stayed home and most small stores remained shuttered. This week, a second, less successful attempt at a general strike threw the government into a tailspin. In San Pedro, only a third of those who labor in the Zona Franca stayed home. Shopkeepers opened their stores after government troops took to the streets.

I met Mojica two days ago. He sat at the lone desk in his union hall and showed me copies of letters he has sent to government officials over the years. "The labor laws in this country are only pieces of paper," the old man said. "Foreign owners laugh at them; our own government ignores them. Those who want to live either fight or leave for New York." (August 2, 1991)

TIJUANA, MEXICO — The Ming Dynasty emperors built the Great Wall of China to keep savage nomads out of their land. This barrier of stone, earth and brick, 25 feet high and 1,500 miles long, took hundreds of years to complete and remains one of the great monuments to human insecurity.

The black corrugated steel barrier separating Mexico from the US is not nearly so impressive: 10 feet high, less than an inch thick, edged with dull spikes and only 7 miles long. It has taken the US Army and Border Patrol three years to erect those seven miles. There are plans for another 7 miles to be added, but no dates have been set.

Yesterday evening, dozens of men, women and children waited in the shadow of the wall for their turn to slip across *El Bordo*, the Tijuana River channel which separates this city of one million from US territory. The border patrol says the wall is meant to slow down drug trafficking, but everyone knows its real purpose is to halt the daily flow of Latin Americans crossing the border illegally to look for work. In 1991 alone, 540,000 people were apprehended by the patrol in the California sector south of San Diego; half of all the arrests along the 2,000-mile border between the US and Mexico are made within these

7 miles. Many of those are repeated apprehensions – the same people recrossing – but it is still an astonishing statistic. Of course, the great irony of this effort to block immigration from Mexico is that the US economy – agribusiness and the service industries in particular – need illegal, low-wage workers to stay competitive, something the nation as a whole is loath to admit.

Recently, the flood of undocumented immigrants has exacerbated racial and ethnic tensions at the local and national level. Many white Americans take the view that the country is now overrun with illegals; in Southern California, there has been an increase in violence against Mexicans and other Central Americans. This week, for example, a Mexican family won a $275,000 insurance settlement from an American family whose son was involved in the shooting to death of their 12-year-old boy. The child, Emilio Jimenez Bejinez, was killed on May 18, 1990. He was crossing the border with his uncle when he was felled by a bullet from a high-powered rifle. The shot came from the house of 21-year-old Leonard Cuen. On that night, Cuen and two friends had been drinking beer and popping pills when they decided to "shoot some aliens." One of the trio, Dwight Pannel, grabbed a rifle and fired at Bejinez from 300 yards. Pannel pleaded guilty to involuntary manslaughter and received a two-year sentence. Now Cuen's family must pay the bill.

According to human rights advocates, this kind of violence is on the rise in the region – and the perpetrators are not always vigilantes. In 1991, the American Friends Service Committee (AFSC) received 405 complaints of physical attacks along the border, most of which were committed by the Border Patrol. Of these complaints, 31 percent were from US citizens or legal residents who had been mistaken for illegal immigrants. Roberto Martinez, who heads the US–Mexico Border Project for the AFSC, reports that 150 people have been either killed or run over by cars while crossing into the US since 1985.

Yesterday, on the Tijuana side, Spanish-language graffiti spelled out in big blue and red letters, "No One Can Deny Us the Legal

Right to Work." In spite of the risks, the people here are fearless and optimistic; the physical reality of this man-made barrier is no real match for the truth of economic deprivation. Near the wall, a half-dozen women from the state of Guerrero waited for a *coyote* to lead them across the border. It had taken them three days and two nights to make the 2,000-mile trip. One older member of the group, her face hidden behind a black jacket, explained to me the purpose of her crossing: "I'm going to see my son in Escondido. He's been there for twenty years. I want to see him one more time before I die."

"That wall doesn't stop anything," said a young, fast-talking *coyote* who was looking for people to take across. "It's not even real steel. A few weeks ago, a car rammed right into it and knocked part of it down.

"Look at those people," he continued, pointing to the mass waiting patiently to cross. "They'll never find a way to stop us. When you have to eat, you must find work." (January 15, 1992)

MATAMOROS, MEXICO – Some of them are in their twenties and still wear diapers. Their spindly arms and legs constantly convulse, and they communicate in bone-chilling shrieks only a parent could hope to understand. Others move and talk normally but possess the minds of seven year olds. Their facial features are flat and listless.

They are called the children of Mallory. At last count there were seventy, all born with birth defects between 1970 and 1977 in this city of 400,000 just across the Rio Grande from Brownsville, Texas. Their mothers all worked while pregnant on the assembly line at Mallory Mexicana S.A., an American-owned electronics factory. The story of these children is tragic proof of the environmental and public health disaster that US corporations have created along the Mexican border in the name of free trade.

For a decade, the Mallory plant produced capacitors for televisions. Opened in 1967, it was one of the first *maquiladora* plants on the Mexican side of the border. At its peak, Mallory ran three shifts and employed as many as 200 women. The ex-employees whose job it was to heat and stir vats of liquid gases claim they worked without respirators or protective clothing and were exposed to dangerous compounds without any special training.

But their health and safety was not a primary concern for the electronics firm. Originally headquartered in Indianapolis, Mallory – like hundreds of other US companies – chose to move across the border to take advantage of Mexico's cheap labor. This became possible in the mid 1960s, after the US and Mexico concluded an experimental free trade agreement reducing tariffs for new factories near the border which used US-made raw materials and exported the finished product back to the States. Since then, nearly 2,000 *maquiladora* plants have opened. Many of these operations have relocated from New York, Chicago, Detroit and other industrial cities, leaving behind thousands of out-of-work garment and electronics workers. By contrast, the *maquiladora* plants are staffed by half a million Mexicans for obvious reasons: what capitalist in his right mind would pay a US worker $7 an hour when he can pay a Mexican $7 a day for the same job?

This huge investment has created an environmental and demographic crisis along the border. There have been unparalleled population explosions in half a dozen Mexican towns because millions have left the countryside looking for work and the country lacks the infrastructure to deal with these fast-growing cities. Also, workplace monitoring is almost nonexistent in Mexico – in 1991, the government spent 48 cents per capita on environmental protection compared with $24.40 in the US – and industrial expansion has resulted in degraded resources and health standards.

A report issued in 1991 by the National Toxic Campaign Fund (NTCF) stated that "Mexico's neighborhoods are being poisoned by industrial toxic chemicals." The environmental group's sampling of the waste water from General Motors' Rimir plant showed 2.8 million parts per billion of xylene had been discharged into the sewer system: a percentage 6,300 times higher than the US drinking water standard.

Xylene, an industrial solvent, can cause lung, liver and kidney damage, as well as brain hemorrhages.

Already, the entire Texas border region has a greater incidence of hepatitis and gastrointestinal diseases than the rest of the state and the nation. A recent University of Texas study showed high levels of liver and gall-bladder cancer for the thirty-three counties along the Rio Grande, the region which supplies much of the drinking water for south Texas and northern Mexico. In 1991, at least ten local babies were born without brains.

This year, President Bush will try once again to ram a free trade agreement with Mexico through Congress. The new agreement is something favored by all of corporate America. With no tariffs between the two countries, US industry is expected to flee to Mexico in ever bigger numbers, leaving more American workers unemployed and turning vast sections of our southern neighbor's territory into an industrial disaster zone. (January 22, 1992)

BROWNSVILLE, TEXAS — If rivers could only talk, the Rio Grande would shriek with bone-chilling wails of people — crime victims really — being doused in acid and left to die.

The Rio Grande begins, innocently enough, as a crystal clear stream in the San Juan mountains of Colorado. The river then meanders the length of New Mexico, snakes east to form the boundary between Texas and Mexico, and eventually empties into the Gulf of Mexico a few miles beyond this dusty border city. Here in the Lower Rio Grande Valley, the river serves as the main source of drinking water for 2 million people in both countries and irrigates a vast stretch of farmland. More than 2,000 miles long, it is one of the great waterways of North America. It is also the most polluted.

Six weeks ago, in a report which received little attention, a national conservation group called American Rivers concluded that the Rio Grande "poses a greater threat to human health than any other river system in North America." The group blamed the pollution on "newly developed industrial plants along the Mexican side of the border," most of them *maquiladoras*, which dump enormous quantities of toxic waste into the river.

American Rivers' findings were shocking but hardly unexpected. Even the American Medical Association has called the US–Mexico border area "a virtual cesspool and breeding ground for infectious disease." If companies like General Motors, Zenith, and Dupont – which operate giant *maquiladoras* – succeed in getting Congress to approve the North American Free Trade Agreement (NAFTA) this year, the river could become the epicenter of the biggest environmental disaster of our age. The American Rivers report hints at the approaching disaster, citing the recent rash of neural tube birth defects in the area. The cause of such birth defects is unknown, but one British study has found links to xylene, the industrial solvent that watchdog groups have discovered at astronomical levels in the sewage lines of some US plants on the Mexican side.

In January 1992, I wrote about infants born with no brains or with deformed brain stems in Brownsville and Matamoros, the twin city on the Mexican side. Since then, these births have increased in number – in one eighteen-month period there were fifty – and received national attention. The Centers for Disease Control ordered a study of US-born affected babies. The results were inconclusive; the CDC did not include Mexican-born children (the group most at risk) in their survey.

Environmentalists suspect that politics tinged the results. The Mexican and US governments have been scrambling to convince a skeptical Congress to pass NAFTA which would gradually eliminate tariffs between the countries and prompt even more US factories to move to low-wage, no-benefit Mexico. Neither former President George Bush nor President Carlos Salinas wants any scandals this year about babies without brains.

Paula Gomez believes there is a cover-up. She is the long-time director of the Brownsville Community Health Center. Two years ago, a radiologist at Pumarejo Hospital in Matamoros showed Gomez infant health records that detailed what she calls "an amazing number of birth defects." Several months later, when pediatrician Carmen Rocco tried to obtain copies of those records for an independent study, hospital authorities refused to cooperate, insisting that there had not been an unusual number of abnormal births. Hermilio Mata Verdinis, who works for the General Motors' Rimir plant in Matamoros, and his wife say their baby died shortly after being born brainless in April 1992. However, the death certificate at the Mexican Social Security Hospital said "natural causes" and the hospital file had no mention of birth defects.

Other aspects of the health disaster along our border are not so easily hidden. Since 1991, childhood cancers in the Brownsville public schools have increased by 230 percent. Public health workers have witnessed a resurgence of infectious diseases long thought to be eradicated. In 1990, for instance, there were fifty-three cases of leprosy along the border, thirty-seven on the Texas side and sixteen on the Mexican side. The cholera epidemic that has been moving steadily north from Peru has reached the Rio Grande; the border towns of Reynosa and Juarez, swollen with Mexicans drawn to the *maquiladoras*, reported their first cases this year. The country's radio stations constantly broadcast warnings about the disease, alerts that are already being heard in south Texas. Locals realize that it is only a matter of time before the disease reaches the States.

Still, American and Mexican executives, fat with greed, trumpet the miracle of free trade. If only the river could speak. (June 10, 1993)

MATAMOROS, MEXICO — A knock on the door in the middle of the night. A jailer administering electric shocks. A body dumped in a river. The stolen election. These are the frightening images of Mexico you will never hear about from a Cancun tourist guide or a Washington politician.

This is the reality Mexicans have endured through sixty-three consecutive years of rule by the Institutional Revolutionary Party (PRI), a group currently enjoying the longest reign of any political party in the world. As our government becomes ever more righteous and angry over human rights violations in distant places like China and Bosnia and Somalia – and in not-so-distant ones like Haiti and Cuba – why the silence from Washington about the virtual police state operating next door? Why is nothing said about the continuing terror, one-party rule and widespread government corruption in Mexico?

Consider the cases of Juan Gutierrez, Anna Maria Guillen and Agapito Gonzalez, three popular leaders in Matamoros, now repressed, in hiding or abroad. Gutierrez is a member of the liberal Revolutionary Democratic Party (PRD) who ran for the state assembly from Matamoros last November on a coalition slate with the conservative Authentic National Party (PAN). Gutierrez and Guillen, who heads the PRD in Matamoros, received a list of the eligible voters the day before the election. They began to check it against the lists from the actual polling stations. In some instances, they found hundreds of voters listed as living on nonexistent streets. In some precincts there were more votes than registered voters.

The night the polls closed, the government stopped the count halfway through and announced it would be resumed in a few days. It was said that the paper ballots were being taken to the state capital. The opposition coalition objected. Hundreds of people surrounded Matamoros's city hall and refused to let the ballots be moved. Police arrived and attacked the protesters. Some protesters (Gutierrez insists they were provocateurs) set fires and in the ensuing chaos the uncounted ballots – half the total vote – were burned. The government declared victory and ordered the arrests of more than fifty opposition leaders on charges which included terrorism, arson, and inciting a riot. Gutierrez, who was not present when the ballots were burned, was jailed for several months. There, according to the government's official National Commission on Human Rights, he was severely beaten by inmates on orders from his jailers.

In Mexico, torture is endemic, in the words of Amnesty

International. In 1990, the Campeche State Bar Association charged that 99 percent of criminal suspects were tortured or ill-treated. President Carlos Salinas de Gortari, who squeaked into office in an election marred by charges of widespread voter fraud, promised he would end abuses by the federal and state police. According to Amnesty International, very little has changed during his term.

In late 1991, US immigration judges began, for the first time, to grant political asylum to Mexicans. Gutierrez's comrade, Guillen, escaped arrest by fleeing to Weslaco, Texas, and is awaiting an asylum hearing. The case of the labor leader Gonzalez is even more remarkable. Gonzalez is the 76-year-old head of the 35,000-member Union of Day Laborers and Industrial Workers in Matamoros. The Matamoros workers earn, on the average, 30 percent more than any other factory workers in the 2,000 plants in various border cities. In December 1990, when the owners wanted to do away with the 40-hour workweek in Matamoros and bring back the 48-hour week prevalent in other border cities, Gonzalez refused. He called a strike, shutting down production for more than a week until the owners relented. A month later, a police helicopter flew to Matamoros from Mexico City. The cops grabbed Gonzalez, threw him in the helicopter, and flew him off to jail on charges of income tax evasion. He remained in prison for six months, after which, having learned his lesson, Gonzalez was released and proceeded to turn over day-to-day operations to his son.

As Congress prepares to vote on the North American Free Trade Agreement, someone should be asking: What kind of government are we doing business with? (June 11, 1993)

NEW YORK, NEW YORK — When Dorca Noemi Diaz spotted the stylish tan skirt hanging from a rack at Macy's, she froze in her tracks. It was as though she'd seen a ghost. "That's it, that's the one," she whispered to her friend.

To anyone else at Macy's last Saturday, the skirt was just another of the thousands of garments for sale at the 34th Street store. To people like Diaz, a 20-year-old factory worker from Honduras, and her friend, Bernie Hartglass, a 62-year-old sample cutter in the city's garment district, the innocuous cloth testifies to the continuing rape of American and foreign workers by manufacturers whose greed pledges allegiance to no flag.

Back in the Chip Choloma Free Trade Zone of Honduras, Diaz used to work on an assembly line for $2.50 a day making that same Leslie Fay skirt. Every day, she and sixty other women on the line produced five hundred of them, while on a second line sixty women turned out five hundred more. Another five assembly lines made dresses.

It's a profitable business. In a single day the 120 women on the two assembly lines cost their boss a grand total of $300, yet they produce – in that one day – skirts that would sell for $40,000 retail. Even if you subtract mark-ups for all the middlemen, shipping costs, overhead charges and taxes, that's still a lot of money. Is it any wonder that Leslie Fay, the second-largest dress manufacturer in the United States, now produces about 80 percent of its clothes in places such as Honduras, Guatemala and other Third World countries? Why should it surprise us that American workers who have toiled tirelessly over the years to make Leslie Fay the rich corporate giant it is now face the extinction of their jobs?

On June 1, 1993, the last 1,700 Leslie Fay workers in the US went on strike – the first strike in company history – in New York, Pennsylvania and other states. They are simply fed up with watching their jobs shipped overseas while desperate workers in Latin America, many of them children, replace them at salaries that don't even reach poverty levels in those countries.

All the plants are in foreign free trade zones, mostly in the Caribbean, where the manufacturers pay neither local taxes nor import duties into the US. In other words, it's welfare for the capitalist – tax subsidies for companies in both the producing and receiving nations. This corporate mugging gets no attention in the daily press. In fact, it is perfectly legal; Leslie Fay and their like are commended and rewarded for being competitive. "It's hard to justify to people who are losing their jobs," admits Michael Freitag, a spokesman for Leslie Fay. "But that's a reality of the local economy. We're saying your job [here] is a dead-end job. This company is not making money [from US production]."

Last month, after Diaz was fired from her factory for trying to organize a union, she came to New York to give spiritual support to Leslie Fay strikers here. Workers in both countries have come to realize that in this much-hyped global marketplace, the only way to survive is by uniting their efforts — just like the bosses and the politicians. (June 10, 1994)

NEW YORK, NEW YORK — Ruth Silber was standing in front of the main library on 42nd Street a week ago when one of New York's Finest ordered her to disperse.

"Why?" asked the 74-year-old woman.

"You're under arrest," the cop barked by way of explanation as he handcuffed her.

The retired legal secretary had been carrying a picket sign in front of the Mexican Consulate and a branch of Chase Manhattan Bank. She was fuming about this Mexico thing — how Chase Manhattan and other US banks are making off with $20 billion of our tax dollars to bail themselves out of the so-called Mexican peso crisis.

So brazen are these banks that Chase, for one, is advocating election fraud in Mexico and openly calling for war. On January 13, a memo by Riordan Roett, a top analyst for Chase Manhattan's Emerging Markets Group, reviewed the year-long Zapatista Indian rebellion in Chiapas and concluded: "While Chiapas, in our opinion, does not pose a fundamental threat to Mexican political stability, it is perceived to be so by many in the investment community. The government will need to eliminate the Zapatistas to demonstrate their effective control of the national territory and of security policy." Several paragraphs later, Roett warns that the government of President

Ernesto Zedillo "will need to consider carefully whether or not to allow opposition victories if fairly won at the ballot box."

The extraordinary memo went unnoticed when it was first publicized by *CounterPunch*, a muckraking Washington newsletter. But after it appeared on the Internet, calls were issued for a boycott of Chase and for protests in New York and San Francisco. The New York picketing turned ugly when a handful of protesters entered Chase's midtown branch and started overturning files. Silber was arrested even though she insists she never entered the bank.

Within weeks of the Roett memo, however, President Zedillo did an about-face in his policy. He broke a year-long truce with the Zapatista rebels and dispatched federal troops to occupy Chiapas. And as soon as Zedillo moved against the Zapatistas, the Mexican stock market and the peso immediately rebounded; when Zedillo backed away from a full war late last week, the market and the peso fell again. The fact is that since the passing of the North American Free Trade Agreement, the US and Mexican economies have become so intertwined that when Mexico sneezes, we catch a cold.

The $50 billion international bailout of the Mexican peso that President Clinton recently engineered without congressional approval — $20 billion of it American money — will go mostly to salvage the risky investments of big American bondholders and Mexican millionaires, not to ease the plight of Mexico's impoverished masses, now poorer than ever. But most outrageous are the incestuous ties between Robert Rubin — Clinton's pointman who is also the Treasury secretary and former president of Goldman, Sachs & Co. — and Mexico's government and corporate elite. While testifying before a congressional committee last month, consumer advocate Ralph Nader reminded Congress that Rubin earned $25 million from Goldman, Sachs in 1992, most of it from his work on the firm's Mexican investments. For example, it was Rubin who got Goldman the contract to handle the $2.3 billion privatization of Mexico's telephone company in 1990. Under Rubin's guidance, the firm also handled the first public offering for Grupo Televisa, Mexico's media giant. In his financial disclosure statement given on joining the Clinton White House, Rubin listed six major Mexican clients of Goldman's with which he had had significant contact. They included Mexico's Finance Ministry and its Central Bank. Now Rubin is leading the bailout negotiations with the very entities for which he once served as financial adviser.

Like the Roett memo, the question of Rubin's conflict of interest is yet to be given a public hearing. For the time being, Wall Street simply mugs Main Street in broad daylight – and cops arrest the nearest 74-year-old woman. (February 21, 1995)

6

HAITI, 1991–94

On September 30, 1991, Jean-Bertrand Aristide, Haiti's first democratically elected president, was overthrown in a bloody army coup led by General Raoul Cedras. For the next three years, despite an ostensible world economic boycott and buttressed by a duplicitous US policy toward Haiti, the coup leaders and the country's tiny mulatto elite retained power while slaughtering several thousand Aristide supporters. I visited the country several times during and after the coup to report on the fight for democracy in this hemisphere's poorest country.

FOR THE FIRST time since last Monday, when an army coup ousted Haiti's young president, the Reverend Jean-Bertrand Aristide, life began to return to normal on the streets of the capital. Thousands of Haitians left their homes to shop or to wait in long lines at gasoline stations.

At the main public hospital in Port-au-Prince, however, there was no escaping the horror of what is happening in this destitute country. The maimed and dying, victims of the latest unrest, overflowed the sprawling wards, covering the dirty floors of the hospital's halls with bloodied bodies. The flies, grime and shortages of everything from beds and bed linens to nurses and doctors seemed to underscore how unimportant the oppressed people of Haiti are to the outside world. In one bed, a young boy stared at the ceiling, a bandage wrapped around his severed calf. In another, a man with a broken leg tossed in agony as a friend tried to comfort him. He had been waiting for almost a week for a doctor to operate on it.

One young doctor, who had been working with little sleep since Sunday, stopped to talk. "We doctors are tired of the killing and the blood," he said. "And now they talk of armies from the outside that will only bring more killing. Already sixty people have died here from gun-shot wounds while we operated on them." Like so many people in this country, the doctor feared being identified.

Less than a mile away at army headquarters, General Raoul Cedras had called a press conference late in the afternoon to deny reports that he was a new dictator. "This is not a coup," the general declared. "It is a correction of the democratic process." When asked why virtually all the radio stations in the country, including the popu-lar Radio Soleil and Radio Lumiere, had been forced off the air by the army in this "correction," Cedras replied: "We are in a very delicate situation. We must prevail on the people to stay calm."

According to Cedras, Aristide had been inciting the people "to attack the rich" and had been violating the constitution in many ways, especially by trying to create a new independent militia. He reminded reporters that at least twenty soldiers had been killed or wounded by Aristide supporters. What he neglected to mention was that Aristide had also decreed a doubling of the minimum wage – to have started last Monday – and had instituted reductions in university fees and in the price of basic food products like flour.

We questioned Cedras on whether this latest coup is giving the army more trouble than anticipated. Unconfirmed reports from outside the capital were that in provinces like Cape Haitian, Cays and Jeremie Haiti's poor are resisting the army and have, in some places, taken over towns. "Some people are involved in urban guerrilla war," Cedras admitted. But he insisted that order was being restored and that "everything is calm in the provinces."

As he spoke in his air-conditioned office across from the presidential palace someone commented on the bullet holes in the ceiling and asked Cedras if he had been attacked in his own office. "What makes you think those are bullet holes?" he responded with a smile. Earlier, Cedras had claimed that he was dragged into the rebellion and that troops had even shot into his office at headquarters when he initially refused to lead the assault on the palace.

Outside, on a street appropriately named John Brown Avenue, a brawny man named Moses talked frankly about the situation. Moses, who has worked in the Dominican Republic, Miami and New York, spoke flawless English. "This man, this general, he lies a lot," Moses said. "We want our president back. The people are waiting." Listening to him speak with such force and conviction, I sensed that the worst is yet to come . . .

NEVER HAVE I seen a people so gripped with terror. One week after the coup, hundreds are dead, and the population of this impoverished nation has been covered by a blanket of fear and silence.

The signs are everywhere: At St Jean Bosco, the church where Aristide became a near-mythic hero among Haiti's poor, the gates to the grounds were locked. A frightened caretaker said that soldiers had been watching the churchgoers for days and that they had fired shots into the Mazda dealership across the street after an Aristide poster was hung in the window. At another church in the more middle-class town of Petionville, the priests have been known to give sermons with strong social messages; yesterday they avoided all mention of politics and the bloody upheaval racking the country. And in the sprawling shantytown neighborhood of La Saline, people backed away in fear when they learned I was a reporter. One youth said, "I don't support either Peter or Paul. I don't have anything to say." Even the prime minister of the country, Rene Preval, was afraid to come out of hiding or to convene his own parliament.

The legislative body decided to meet anyway. Senators and deputies began to gather early in the morning to decide who would run the country. They met throughout the day. US Ambassador Alvin Adams emerged from a closed-door session with senators shortly before the 7 P.M. curfew, after which gunfire underscored the fact that there has been no solution to the "constitutional crisis."

"The army doesn't want power. It just wants to get rid of Aristide," Dejean Belizaire, the president of the senate, told a throng of reporters from around the world. Belizaire wore a gray pinstriped suit and spoke slowly and deliberately. This is a politican who wants to stay alive. "We will reach a final position" was his only comment when asked who will run the government. He has asked Cedras to guarantee the safety of the prime minister. According to Belizaire, lawmakers were considering naming a Supreme Court justice to replace Aristide and calling elections in ninety days.

The truth is that lawmakers here have a big problem. If they choose a provisional president to replace the ousted Aristide – thereby tacitly supporting the coup – they risk world condemnation, a continued boycott by other countries, and a dangerous situation at home. "Haiti can't survive more than a week or two with this embargo," explained Jean-Claude Roy, a human-rights activist. "The people will start rioting when the goods run out." But if parliament tries to bring Aristide back, it risks angering the army further. And if Aristide returns, his supporters among the poor may explode in revenge against those who ousted him.

There can be no doubt that Aristide's many speeches in which he called on Haiti's poor to demand justice from the rich frightened not only top business people but also the country's middle-class professionals. For example, in a speech Aristide gave shortly after returning from the United Nations before the coup, he appeared to support "necklacing" – a form of vigilante justice in which the poor burn their enemies by placing scalding tires around their necks.

Roy was critical of the international community for not "investigating things well before supporting Aristide." Now, he feels, it's payback time. "The winds are changing. The world is seeing now some of the horrible things Aristide did." Roy represents the concerns of the tiny middle class.

But when you drive through the destitute slums of this capital city, in this the poorest country in the western hemisphere, you can understand some of Aristide's anger and his impatience with the wealthy classes. Once this nation had so much hope for the young priest; instead of healing, his election ended up dividing further.

Maybe we must come to accept that when the poor of Haiti rise up, their justice will not be a delicate or pretty sight. Their wounds are too deep, the scars of their oppression too painful, to lay quiet for too long . . .

ARISTIDE, THE RADICAL priest of the poor, was officially replaced as president yesterday by a unanimous vote of the Haitian parliament. His successor is Joseph Nerette, a frail-looking Supreme Court judge who walked into the National Assembly surrounded by soldiers, sporting the most bewildered look I have ever seen on the face of a national leader.

The meeting of parliament had been scheduled for 10 A.M. It began at 3:30 P.M. because it took so long to get a quorum. Legislators talked a lot about democracy and about protecting the constitution as they voted to impeach Aristide and Prime Minister Preval. That they voted with armed and impatient soldiers surrounding the building seemed not to matter. That the night before those same soldiers had tried to storm an OAS meeting at the airport — during which US officials tried in vain to negotiate Aristide's return — seemed a distant memory.

The guess here is that it will be a long while before Aristide returns to Haiti. He now joins Allende of Chile, Arbenz of Guatemala, Goulart of Brazil and Bosch of the Dominican Republic in the pantheon of Latin American leaders overthrown because they were too popular and too radical for the rich elites of their countries. (October 6–9, 1991)

BACK IN 1980, scores of boats overflowing with Cubans began appearing off the Florida Keys.

Between May and August — traveling in everything from rickety dinghies to sleek power boats to lumbering cargo ships — 125,000 *marielitos* reached US shores. Once here, they merely had to utter the magic words "Fidel Castro" and, presto, our government embraced them as refugees.

President Jimmy ("Human Rights") Carter quickly set up camps for the *marielitos* in such out-of-the-way places as Fort Chaffee, Arkansas, Fort Indiantown Gap, Pennsylvania, and Fort McCoy, Wisconsin. Private agencies were offered anywhere from $300 to $1,000 per Cuban to resettle the refugees in new homes. Congress passed a bill reimbursing local governments for the costs of welfare, medical aid and housing assistance for the new arrivals. By September 1980, the government had resettled 105,000 Cubans. But for several thousand others — those suspected of crimes back home — it would be many years of waiting, rioting and even hostage-taking before they too were released into the general population.

When thousands of refugees from Vietnam, Cambodia and Laos arrived here in the late 1970s after the Vietnam War, the same red-carpet treatment was given to them. Since 1975, more than 1 million Asian refugees, most from those three war-torn countries, have been permitted to stay in the US: an average of 60,000 a year. In the more recent past, the last five years of Gorbachev's democratic experiment in the Soviet Union has brought a whopping 160,000 Soviet citizens to our country as political refugees.

But what about the Haitians who lived under the brutal rule of the Duvalier family until 1986 and endured a succession of military dictators, assassinations and massacres? Between 1981 and August 1991, more than 24,000 Haitians were caught by the US Coast Guard trying to get into our country the same way the *marielitos* did. Of those, only twenty-eight were granted refugee status. The rest were shipped back under an agreement with dictator Baby Doc Duvalier. The architect of that interdiction program, lest we forget, was Rudy Giuliani, who was then with the Justice Department.

Six months ago, Aristide was overthrown in a bloody coup in which the army killed an estimated 1,500 citizens and jailed more than 3,000. Military terror against Aristide's Lavalas movement has continued steadily ever since. Even the politicians nominally in charge of the latest dictatorship are not safe. Last October, soldiers opened fire on the parliament building because the legislature wasn't moving quickly enough to officially impeach Aristide. More recently, soldiers broke into a meeting of government leaders, killed the bodyguard of a possible candidate for prime minister, and roughed up the candidate himself. The ton-tons Macoutes have returned. An independent press has been silenced.

The fact of the matter is that today a bunch of thugs in uniform are illegally running Haiti against the will of its people and despite condemnation from the international community. The terror is so great that Haitians are fleeing in unheard-of numbers: in the four months since the coup, 15,000 have been picked up by the US Coast Guard; who knows how many have drowned.

For its part, the Bush administration has decided to go before the US Supreme Court to argue that most Haitians are leaving their country for economic reasons, that the international boycott against Haiti has placed the poorest country in this hemisphere in even more desperate shape. How to explain this blatant disregard for human rights? Some say our country is in a deep recession and can't afford more refugees. The statistics paint a more nuanced landscape: Congress has placed a limit for 1992 of 61,000 Russian refugees and 6,000 other Eastern Europeans, while the ceiling for Latin America – which undoubtedly has more poverty and political repression than Russia and Eastern Europe – is 3,500.

The truth is obvious; in his racist disregard for Haiti's plight, George Bush is no different from a succession of US presidents. For nearly sixty years after African slaves expelled their French masters and won independence in 1804, Haiti was considered a revolutionary and subversive example which Washington long resisted recognizing. Only in 1862, after the Confederate states seceded, did the US establish formal relations. US marines landed in Haiti in 1915 and occupied the country as its lords until 1934, retaining financial control until the late 1940s.

Some might call this ancient history, irrelevant to the plight of the thousands of refugees now at Guantanamo Naval Base. They would choose to believe that our calculated neglect of Haitian suffering inexplicably fell from the sky and did not sprout from the New World soil that African slaves once made rich with cotton and sugar. (February 5, 1992)

IT WAS NEARLY eight months ago that the Coast Guard cutter *Hamilton* plucked the rickety wooden boat crammed with Marie, her husband Pierre and ninety other desperate Haitians out of the sea.

They'd been tossing for two days in the blustery waters of the Windward Passage when the sleek Coast Guard ship, stars and stripes fluttering in the breeze, intercepted their small boat and whisked them off to Guantanamo Naval Base. After a few weeks in Guantanamo with thousands of others who had fled from the bloody dictatorship in their country, Marie and Pierre were among the few lucky ones granted entrance to the US as political refugees. In June, they moved to New York to live with Marie's sister.

The story they tell of life in Haiti postcoup is tragic but typical.

On May 9, Pierre and Marie fled St Mark, which lies thirty miles north of Port-au-Prince. A few weeks earlier, Marie was chased from her stall in the village marketplace by the *zenglendos*, criminals who act with the support of the army, for selling T-shirts with the deposed president's picture on them. Pierre, a construction worker by trade, had been the leader of a neighborhood committee loyal to Aristide. The night they left, Pierre was holding a meeting of the committee when a government representative burst into the room, ordered them to disperse, and warned them Aristide would never come back to power. A few minutes later, soldiers surrounded the house and started shooting. Pierre escaped, and he and Marie then hid from the army for a week before finding a boat that was scheduled to leave the country from the nearby town of Mt Rouis on May 18. They left behind three children, ages three, ten and twelve. "We're here physically," Pierre said in a quivering, soft voice, "but in my heart, I'm still with my children."

Today, Marie and Pierre will not budge from the sofa in front of the television in their simply decorated house in Brooklyn for fear of missing one minute of the inauguration of Bill Clinton. Even though they understand little English, the couple from the poorest and most forsaken nation in our hemisphere will cling to every word spoken by the new president of the richest and most powerful nation on earth for a clue to the future of their fellow Haitians.

A few weeks ago, they were sure Clinton's inauguration would be one of the great celebrations of their lives. Now, like so many others in this country, they feel duped, disillusioned and demeaned. For millions of Americans, a broken Clinton campaign promise may mean a higher tax bill, or a delay in getting that new job, or even that new car. But for Haitian émigrés like Marie and Pierre it can mean a mother tortured, a sister raped, a father jailed, a brother killed, a nephew drowned. As Clinton takes the oath to defend our democracy today, a flotilla preapproved by the new commander-in-chief is already blockading the hopes of millions in Haiti for the one right we take for granted: to freely elect our leaders.

Bill Clinton, the candidate, told the American people he would revoke George Bush's policy of sending the Haitians home. His words were meant more for the ears of black voters than for Haitian boat people. As soon as he got the necessary votes, Clinton reverted to the policies of Bush – no, worse than Bush. Whereas Bush deployed only a few Coast Guard cutters, Clinton has called out a fleet and backed it up with airplanes. In one of his initial acts as president, Clinton has created a floating Berlin Wall around the first black republic in the Americas. Instead of blockading the generals who killed democracy, he is blockading the victims from whom it was taken.

"We were very glad at first when we heard Clinton speak because he held out hope to us for Haiti," said Marie, a large, attractive woman with a resonant voice. "Now, I don't understand what he is doing. If there is no restoration of Aristide, there is no peace in Haiti.

"Maybe, he'll change once he gets in office," she added optimistically.

And maybe he won't. (January 20, 1993)

DESPITE AN INTERNATIONAL embargo against trade with Haiti's postcoup government, major US companies such as Sears Roebuck, J.C. Penney and WalMart are still stocking their stores with goods made by Haitian workers who toil for as little as fourteen cents an hour.

This information about life in Haiti since the coup of September 30, 1991, is revealed in a new report issued by a group of American labor leaders who visited the country in March 1993. The nearly 200-page document by the National Labor Committee in Support of Worker and Human Rights in Central America is a devastating indictment of our government's hypocritical policy – first under Bush and now under President Clinton – toward Haiti. Among the allegations in the report:

- Although Haiti is the poorest country in the western hemisphere and has the lowest minimum wage (twenty-two cents an hour), workers employed by US-owned companies or by companies that supply US retailers sometimes earn even less than that, often as little as fourteen cents an hour. Workers typically spend more than half their daily pay, about seventy-four cents, on transportation and lunch.

- Employee benefits are nonexistent. The army generals have looted the bank accounts of the national pension office, and no companies – this includes American-owned firms – are currently paying into the government's health insurance system. The public hospitals have gotten so bad that "you must bring your own sheets and purchase your own food while you are there. Often more than one person is in a bed."

- While 90 percent of industry in Haiti is American-owned, not a single collective bargaining agreement with any union exists. Since the coup, unions have been broken and their leaders arrested or sent underground.

One of the companies singled out by the report, Vetex, is a Haitian–American venture which was found to be making children's clothes under the Silver Unicorn, KV Kids and Electric Kids labels for several major firms, including Sears. A Sears spokesman denied that the retail giant had had any dealings with Haitian companies since the coup. When told that hundreds of items of children's clothing with the Sears label had been spotted by the American labor delegation at the Vetex firm in Haiti, the spokesman replied that Sears "expects strict adherence to applicable local and US laws" by companies that produce for its label. "Until you called," he admitted, "we weren't aware of this."

The international garment industry in recent years has become as shadowy and elusive as the CIA. Figuring out who owns which firm and who provides the product to a retailer has become the stuff of real detective work. Shifting ownerships and company titles have provided fertile ground for hustling middlemen trying to make a quick buck or for giant retailers seeking to avoid responsibility for the working conditions of those who produce their goods. In Haiti, where government-sponsored terror and murder have been the rule for so long, this type of corporate irresponsibility should be branded as what it is: criminal negligence. (May 19, 1993)

JAMES GREGORY PULLEY kept staring into the full-length mirror, fidgeting with his beret. In all the war-ravaged infernos of this world, places like Bosnia and Somalia and Cambodia, that sky-blue beret with the insignia of the United Nations stands for moral authority, the dream of a world at peace.

But the blue beret has never been known to stop a bullet. The peacemakers who wear it have been buried far too often in our time. Maybe that's why Pulley, a hardened 25-year veteran of the US Special Forces, still seemed to be getting used to his hat around noon yesterday in the VIP lounge of the Port-au-Prince airport.

Half an hour later, an advance group arrived of what soon will be the hundreds of UN troops that Pulley will command. This first group – twenty-six US noncombat soldiers and six Canadian police – landed in a Miami air charter as throngs of Haitians milled around the airport. The arrival of these first international soldiers was the clearest signal yet to the clique of military officers who two years ago overthrew Haiti's democratically elected president in a bloody coup that the end of their power is around the corner. As part of a UN-brokered agreement reached at Governors Island in June, Aristide will return to office on October 30, 1993, and General Raoul Cedras, the coup leader, will resign. That, at least, is the plan; but many of the officers, especially the city's police chief, Michel Francois, the real power behind the coup, have said that they do not plan to step down.

Pulley, who has spent his whole career in troubled Latin American countries in what Washington calls nation-building projects, now has probably his toughest assignment of all: helping to return democracy to this beleaguered nation. "There is no combat role for us," Pulley explained.

Another 200 US Navy personnel will arrive from Puerto Rico

over the weekend and a total of 600 US troops will set up camp before Aristide's arrival. They will be joined by more Canadian and French police. But the troops will consist largely of engineers, medics and combat support personnel who will be stationed here for six months to help build roads and clinics and do other infrastructure work. And US military instructors will help retrain and professionalize the Haitian army.

"We do, of course, have plans to protect ourselves," Pulley said emphatically, an indirect warning to the *attachés* – the armed thugs who in recent months have assassinated or beaten Aristide's supporters in violent incidents around the country – not to mess with UN troops. While the first UN arrivals were not even carrying sidearms, a crew of Americans in plain clothes with heavy duffel bags strapped to their shoulders – clearly not filled with romance novels – rode shotgun on the detachment.

Many people are worried about what will happen to Aristide when he arrives in Haiti. Will he become another Benigno Aquino, the anti-Marcos Filipino opposition leader who was shot to death as he arrived at Manila Airport more than a decade ago? Before he was ousted in the 1991 coup, Aristide already had been the target of several failed assassination attempts. Haiti, after all, is not known for peaceful transitions: in the second decade of this century alone, seven Haitian presidents were assassinated or removed from office. One was blown up in his palace. Another, Vilbrun Guillaume Sam, was dragged through the streets by a mob on July 28, 1915, and dismembered in front of the American *chargé*, R.B. Davis.

"I think everyone is concerned," said US Embassy spokesman Stanley Schrager, "but we hold the Haitian Army responsible for the protection of President Aristide." The State Department is right now training sixty Haitians to be Aristide's bodyguards. That amounts to a mere twenty men in three shifts a day. What of all the other members of Aristide's cabinet and government? Who will protect them from intimidation or murder?

Halfway around the world in Somalia, the number of US dead is mounting and Americans want out. In Haiti, to which we have much deeper ties and much greater responsibility, the question may soon be: Is Washington willing to risk American lives to defend Haitian democracy? (October 7, 1993)

HAITI TOOK A step back into its vicious past yesterday. Masquerading under a new label, the ton-tons Macoutes of former dictator Papa Doc Duvalier were back in the streets, calling a general strike – and enforcing it with naked terror.

On any normal morning, Delmas Street is clogged to a crawl with the crush of people, cars, and Tap-Taps – those rainbow-colored pick-up trucks and vans that haul thousands of Haitians, packed like sweating sardines, to their jobs or to downtown markets. But yesterday, with only three weeks to go before the scheduled return of ousted President Jean-Bertrand Aristide, Port-au-Prince was a ghost town. Hardly anyone went to work. In all of the downtown area no one opened a store. Only journalists with big "TV" letters taped to their cars and the occasional ambulance or army vehicle dared go out. Everyone else obeyed the guys with the guns. Carloads of them crisscrossed town, brandishing rifles and pistols and ordering motorists off the streets.

The group responsible for the day's events calls itself the Front for the Advancement of the Haitian People, or FRAPH – a sparkling new facade for Duvalier's enforcers, who have been trying to repackage their image of late. Operating out of a headquarters only a block from the national palace, these plain-clothes thugs continue to shoot, beat and intimidate Aristide's followers and the appointees of the new transitional government.

With United Nations observers and troops pouring into the country during the past few weeks to prepare the way for Aristide's October 30 return, the military is giving tacit support to thousands of *attachés*, police auxiliaries who are followers of FRAPH. This is how they work: on Delmas Street near the iron market yesterday morning, a group of American reporters including myself drove past a white sedan. Inside the sedan were five men, several with Uzis between their legs. When our driver tried to speed away, the white sedan gave chase and forced us to stop. One man in the front seat angrily questioned our Haitian driver in Creole, while the guys in the back seat stroked their weapons. They demanded to know if we had taken photos of them – we had not – and warned us to stay off Delmas Street.

We pretended to take their advice until they were out of sight. The strike, however, enforced by fear, was sadly successful. "Just because our businesses are closed doesn't mean we support the strike," said Genevieve, a Delmas Street merchant who had been threatened with violence if she opened her shop. Who can question her decision to stay closed? Two years ago, I covered a general strike called by labor unions in the neighboring Dominican Republic. The government opposed it, and on the morning of the strike soldiers were posted at every gas station and on every commuter bus to protect those who chose to work. In contrast, Haitian soldiers and police stayed hidden in their barracks yesterday. They turned the streets over to the thugs.

Even as local authorities laid low, more UN troops – this time twenty-seven Royal Canadian mounted police, all heavily armed – arrived on a commercial plane, and an additional 600 US soldiers will follow by boat starting this weekend. But while the UN prepares for the showdown over Aristide's return, FRAPH and the generals who led the coup have made it clear that they are not ready to give up power. Every time a UN soldier falls in Somalia, the Macoutes in Haiti become more filled with bravado.

From the streets to the halls of government, the mad power struggle continues. You have a pro-Aristide mayor, Evans Paul, who was reinstated some weeks ago but is afraid to go to his City Hall office. He sleeps in a different house each night to avoid assassination by the *attachés*. Then there is Emile Jonnassaint, who was named president of the Supreme Court after the coup two years ago. Aristide's prime minister, Robert Malval, has ordered his retirement, but Jonnassaint refuses. This week the dismissed Supreme Court president thumbed his nose at Aristide's transitional government and opened the court's new term. And who was front and center at the opening ceremony? None other than General Raoul Cedras, the leader of the coup. And yesterday, the pro-Aristide defense minister, who is supposedly Cedras's boss, publicly reprimanded the general for his flagrant meddling in politics. But Cedras pays him no mind. The defense minister, after all, does not command an army.

Under the UN-brokered agreement reached in June, Cedras must resign by next Friday and so must Police Chief Michel Francois, the power behind the coup. But Francois, a mysterious man who shuns interviews and does not like to have his picture taken, has boasted that he will stay.

"Political power comes from the barrel of a gun," declared Mao Ze Dong, the Chinese Communist leader, nearly a half century ago. For no place on earth is that more true than for Haiti. (October 8, 1993)

THEY ARRIVED IN large groups, stepping gingerly around giant puddles in the road to avoid splattering mud on freshly pressed Sunday clothes: bright-eyed children skipping with laughter; teenage girls brimming with confidence; frail old women still filled with spirit; strapping young men with smooth faces and quiet discipline. They poured out from the narrow alleys of the rocky hilltop slum called Rue Tire-Masse – an area of the capital nearly inaccessible except to four-wheel-drive vehicles – and filled the church to capacity. Wherever you went yesterday morning throughout this largely Catholic nation, you encountered similar scenes.

As in the American civil rights movement, churches have played a key role in the Haitian resistance campaign. Haitian democracy first gained strength in religious meeting places. The parish churches kept working in obscurity through the darkest days of the Duvalier dictatorship, despite repeated massacres and coups by different factions of the country's elite. They ran schools, dispensed food and cared for the sick. Scores of foreign priests and missionaries who came to work here over the years – men like the Reverend Rene Giroux, the Canadian pastor at St Michel's – saw the country's grinding poverty and sought to use the church as an agent of change. They were joined in this effort by a generation of militant young Haitian priests who came of age in the last years of the Duvalier terror and believed churches to be the only places where Haitians could gather and speak freely without persecution.

It was in the context of this radical church movement, known throughout Latin America as liberation theology, that a young priest named Jean-Bertrand Aristide first gained a following among the poor in the late 1980s. Some have tried to discredit Aristide and his movement as being nothing more than a Communist front, a charge made against the Reverend Martin Luther King Jr twenty years ago. But Aristide is nothing of the kind. He is only as radical as the conditions that created him. Even Gilbert Mews, scion of Haiti's richest family, has admitted to me that Lavalas, Aristide's political movement, gained wide popularity because the country's rich had thumbed their noses at the poor for so long. The parish churches never did.

There are stark differences between poor churches like St Michel or St Jean Bosco and the more prosperous ones in upper-class Petionville. At St Michel, the main musical instrument used is the African drum; in Petionville, it's either the organ or the guitar. In St Michel and other poor parishes, the songs, sermon and prayers are all in Creole, the language of the majority; in Petionville, they are sung and spoken in French, the language of the elite.

These religious distinctions now carry real political meaning. There is only one Creole translation of the Catholic Church's Book of Readings. It is used by scores of priests, has a decidedly social content and was written by a Haitian priest named William Smarth, who has been in hiding from the army for some time. Smarth is a key Aristide supporter. The words of many classic psalms and hymns have been changed, and verses which contain hidden political messages in support of Aristide have been added by the people themselves.

At yesterday's morning service, for instance, the church's youth choir opened with a mournful melody to the beat of the conga: "My body is torn and causes me to reflect / How the little people have to suffer!" Later, the melody and the words turned upbeat. The choir members began undulating to the rhythm. Their voices rose: "We must make the Earth change / With you, Lord, we will enter the combat / Give us the strength to struggle."

In his sermon, Giroux never mentioned Aristide, but his words were clear. "You don't have a job," he said. "You don't have a house to live in. If there is sickness, you need a place for medical care. We need a politics that will address the needs of the people. And that is what October 30 means."

Gradually, the choir's songs began to address directly the terror of the military: "If a country has problems / Is that a reason to tolerate criminals? / If a country has problems / Is that a reason to say Haiti is finished?" By the end of the service, the tone and content of the singing were openly defiant: "Be aware, be aware, be aware / We need to be prudent / Because they are everywhere / If we are not aware / They will overwhelm us."

As the people filed out of church, some still humming the music, you could see in the rejuvenated St Michel parishioners the face of a new Haiti still awaiting its rebirth. No army terror will ever kill faith like that – which is why so many powerful people, both in Washington and here, still fear the return of the priest. (October 18, 1993)

THE NINE-PAGE confidential memo is written in French and addressed to Jean-Claude (Baby Doc) Duvalier, the Haitian dictator ousted in a popular uprising in 1986. Though dated November 1993, it was just unearthed by *CounterPunch*, the muckraking newsletter of the Institute for Policy Studies in Washington. The memo's author is a one-time Washington lobbyist whose firm represented the interests of the Duvalier government in the early 1980s. But this writer was no run-of-the-mill lobbyist. He was not only a partner in a powerful Washington law firm, but also the vice chairman of the Democratic National

Committee who went on to become party chairman and a major force in Bill Clinton's presidential victory. He is Commerce Secretary Ronald Brown. While a partner in Patton, Boggs & Blow, Brown represented Haiti from 1982 until just before Baby Doc's overthrow.

What's so important about a 10-year-old memo?

Consider these recent statistics: yesterday, four dead Haitian boat people washed up on a south Florida beach; last Wednesday, twelve prodemocracy activists were massacred by soldiers just north of Port-au-Prince; two weeks ago, peasant leader Luckner Elle was grabbed by seventeen armed men, shot to death, and publicly hanged. On the third anniversary of the inauguration of Jean-Bertrand Aristide, the terror in Haiti continues while the world community fiddles. The Brown memo reveals why it's been so difficult to get the US government to squarely oppose Haiti's thugs – they have friends in high places.

Here is some of what Brown reported to Baby Doc:

> Despite the unfair image of Haiti by the American media, and despite the opposition expressed by some members of Congress, it is certain that today . . . a growing number of people – both members of Congress and government officials – stand ready to defend the interests of Haiti. This . . . is essentially due to the work of our Washington team . . ..
>
> We continue to pay a great deal of attention to the Black Caucus and to other "liberal" members of Congress . . . [who] are now, thanks to our efforts, ready to help. Although some of them continue to make negative comments about Haiti, all, without exception, have proved to be cooperative on the issue of aid.

Brown was reporting on his success in getting Congress to say one thing but do another. On foreign aid, he proved more than worth his firm's $150,000 annual retainer. While he represented Haiti, annual US assistance increased from $35 million to $55 million. And, although Amnesty International had openly accused the Duvalier regime of torture, detentions without trial and disappearances, not a word of concern was expressed about human rights violations.

Brown also used his position as a Democratic party honcho to get things done for his client. In the memo, written at the start of the 1984 presidential campaign, he reminds Duvalier that "while we've always maintained excellent relations with the government of President Reagan, we've set out to establish personal contacts with virtually all of the Democratic candidates, thereby ensuring access to the White House regardless of who wins in 1984 . . . . My current role as deputy chairman of the Democratic National Committee has served us well."

Ten years later, you have to wonder what role Brown plays in the two-headed Clinton administration policy, which condemns the military dictatorship publicly but refuses to impose a full boycott to topple it. His press secretary, Carol Hamilton, claims the cabinet member "has not been consulted nor has he weighed in on any of the decisions that have impacted on Haiti."

Meanwhile, time is running out for Aristide and Haiti. Even if he returns to power soon, only two years remain in his term, and he can't succeed himself. The insiders may have already won. (February 9, 1994)

NEXT TIME YOU run on to the field with your company softball team, check the ball. Does it have labels like Comet or Gold Star, some of the brand names of Star Sports Inc.? Or Dunlop or Worth Inc., the country's largest softball producer? If so, chances are good that the ball was made in Haiti and was one of the 2.5 million softballs and 678,000 baseballs imported last year from that nation.

Then consider this: By the most conservative estimate of human-rights observers, more than 110 Haitians were murdered and 37 were kidnapped in the capital of Port-au-Prince during the first three months of this year in a new wave of terror by that country's military thugs. In the countryside, where the repression is even worse, human-rights observers are banned.

This week, the *Miami Herald* reported the story of one victim, Oman Desanges, a supporter of ousted Haitian President Jean-Bertrand Aristide. Desanges tried to escape the terror last year as a boat refugee and was picked up by the US Navy. He applied for political asylum at Guantanamo Naval Base in Cuba but was shipped back to Port-au-Prince, a common fate for thousands of Haitian refugees. On January 24, a group of armed men came to Desanges's house in the Martissant section of Port-au-Prince and took him to the police station for questioning. The next day his family found his body. Half of his face had been cut away and his stomach slit open.

While the Organization of American States and Aristide keep calling for a total trade embargo to topple the illegal regime of dictator General Raoul Cedras, the Clinton administration is doing just the opposite. It is allowing *more* trade with Haiti. In 1993, 64 US companies imported $154 million in goods from Haiti, a 44 percent increase from 1992! Three quarters of the imports came here duty free, despite reports that Haitian workers earn less than $1 a day and that their unions are persecuted. These figures were revealed in a new report by the National Labor Committee Education Fund in Support of Worker and Human Rights in Central America.

Worst among the US firms were the sporting goods companies. Haiti was once the major baseball and softball producer in the world. After the coup three years ago, several companies, such as Rawlings, pulled out. But ball production still thrives on the island. That's because other big firms, like Wilson, who have sold their factories, continue to buy softballs from independent vendors based locally. Others, like Tennessee-based Worth Inc. and Miami-based Star Sports, just stayed in Haiti. "We could've pulled out," said Fred Bryan, president and chief executive officer of Worth, "but we don't run when there's trouble. They [the government] don't bother us and we don't bother them. The only efficient unit in the country that has some degree of training is the military. Remember, the US trained them."

Every few months, President Clinton or Vice President Gore trots Aristide into the Oval Office, smiles for the photographers, and repeats the stock slogans about how the US still backs Haiti's only democratically elected president. Clinton and Gore are outright liars.

In Florida right now, Cuban exiles are training in paramilitary camps to fight Fidel Castro's regime while federal authorities turn their backs; a Cuban radio station and a television station, financed by the US government, beam their messages to the Cuban émigré population; and Cuban boat people are routinely welcomed with open arms. That is what you call a genuine show of support from Washington. In contrast, US policies toward Haiti have been characterized by racist neglect and duplicitous actions. We have read much in the press – most of it planted by the CIA – about how unstable and radical Aristide is. My guess is that Aristide has not been radical enough. He should have moved out of Washington a long time ago, away from false friends in the State Department and the White House who calmly call for compromise while his followers are being massacred in the streets. (April 20, 1994)

BILL CLINTON, WHO thought Vietnam was wrong twenty-five years ago, now seeks to convince America that Haiti is right. "It is time we act," Clinton said last night, to "stop the brutal atrocities" of the Haitian dictators.

Clinton was determined to make a show of his bravery and moral certitude in the face of public and congressional opposition to this deadly exercise. The address to the nation was nothing more than a horrid and hypocritical infomercial: horrid because sending soldiers into Haiti is as wrong as it was in Vietnam or Grenada or Panama or the countless other times the nation has sent fresh-faced young men off to rearrange some country; hypocritical because our government never wanted Jean-Bertrand Aristide, the man the invasion will restore to power next week, to occupy the presidential office in the first place. During the three long years in which Haiti's thugs killed more than 3,000 people, our support for Aristide was always lukewarm.

When Clinton asserted that "the nations of the world have tried every possible way" to remove the dictators, he apparently forgot that it took more than two years before our government joined the international embargo against the military regime. The White House and the State Department kept pressuring Aristide to make concessions to the thugs, all the while allowing American companies to continue operations there. As late as June, during the last of my several trips to Haiti since the coup, I found that our government was employing more than 7,000 Haitians a day to fix roads and build irrigation ditches. This in a country that is supposed to be under total embargo.

Imagine if the US government were paying to fix roads in Saddam Hussein's Iraq or Fidel Castro's Cuba. If the Clinton administration is now willing to invade Haiti, it is because the democracy movement Aristide once represented with such life and vigor is nearly dead. So many Aristide supporters have been killed in the terror of the past three years that his movement has been virtually decapitated. If he returns next week, there will be less than two years left in his term of office and most of that will occur under US occupation. Worst of all, Aristide has already agreed to so many concessions in his program that his power is effectively broken.

But don't believe me: listen to the World Bank and other major international lending institutions. In a meeting with international bankers on August 26 in Paris, Aristide's officers put forward their economic plan. According to that plan, Aristide has agreed to cut the number of public employees in half, to keep the minimum wage low, to privatize as many government-owned agencies and companies as possible, to immediately abolish all import duties except for a few staple foods, and to actively promote foreign investment. He has also pledged to allow the more conservative Haitian parliament a greater role in affairs of state. In short, the radical priest who once defined his peaceful, democratic revolution by how well it attacked Haiti's awesome poverty, has now become a reformed free-market, business-oriented leader.

No wonder Bill Clinton has suddenly become decisive about Haiti. (September 16, 1994)

7

CUBA, 1994

In the summer of 1994, thousands of Cubans fled their island country in small boats, rafts and inner tubes headed toward the Florida shores. I traveled to Miami, Key West and Havana to report on the flotilla of refugees and to examine what this massive exodus meant for the future of Cuba and for American attitudes toward immigration.

VICTOR RODRIGUEZ HAD waited eighteen years to see his first-born son. Now he stood in line, propped on crutches, with his younger son, Anthony, patiently counting down the last few hours before the long-anticipated reunion. The site of the meeting was the INS's Krome Detention Center on the outskirts of Miami, a gleaming port city which has become the new crossroads of Latin America.

Rodriguez left Cuba in 1976 after spending years as a political prisoner. "I was opposed to Castro from the beginning," he explained. "I used to tell my friends, 'Communism is a tall tale and a lie; wait till you see people starving from it.'" His eldest son, a teenager at the time, decided to stay behind to care for his ailing grandmother. A few years ago, after his grandmother's death, Victor Ray Rodriguez Jr decided to join his father and Anthony, whom he had never met, in the US. What he didn't count on was an unpublicized aspect of our country's refugee policy toward Cuba. Despite the official quota of 20,000 visas a year for Cuban immigrants, Washington only grants around 3,000. Cubans who want permission to enter the States legally are forced, ultimately, to risk death at sea to make their escape. Victor Jr left on a tiny raft and sailed all the way to Florida, where he was caught and thrown into Krome. Victor Sr saw his son's name on a list of detainees published in the *Miami Herald* and came to Krome to collect him.

Bill Clinton, embarrassed by the negative publicity his administration has received on its unequal treatment of Cuban and Haitian refugees, is trying desperately to prove that our country is not racist in its immigration policy (which, of course, it is). He has, therefore, decided to treat the Cubans like the Haitians; in other words, no more automatic entry into the States with green cards and welfare benefits. This policy, too, has backfired. "We didn't want the Cubans to be brought down to the level of bad treatment of the Haitians," said Rolande Dorancey, former head of the Haitian Refugee Center. "We wanted the Haitians to get full equality. Now, we are both suffering."

On the Straits of Florida, a flotilla of rafts full of Cuban refugees was taxing the resources of the Coast Guard. Meanwhile, Middle

America was feeling increasingly uncertain about how to respond to this new wave of immigrants. Two nights ago, I flew over the raft-ridden sea with Tom Puccio, an ex-New Yorker whose Italian grandparents had been processed at Ellis Island. Puccio's conflicted reaction to the boat people paddling to shore near his new home in south Florida is, perhaps, indicative of the nation's attitude. "I used to sit home in front of the television and think, send all those goddamn people back where they came from," he said. "But when you see these people risking their lives just to get out of that country, you end up rooting for them to make it and you figure, our country has to be able to help them some way."

While Puccio and the rest of us grappled with the implications and imperatives of our country's immigrant heritage, Victor Rodriguez clutched his son's Cuban birth certificate as he waited in line. That morning Victor Jr had called from Krome. At least his father knew that he was okay. He had been one of the lucky ones. Unlike the Cubans still out at sea, he wouldn't be sent to Guantanamo . . .

IT WAS JUST after 11:30 A.M. when the *Grand Slam* pulled within a few feet of a rowboat in the waters off Key West. We were 24 miles out in a 42-foot fishing boat, and the men in the makeshift craft we'd just overtaken were thrilled to see us. Over the roar of our engine, I yelled to them in Spanish that we had extra water and soda and a few life vests. "We've been out here three days," screamed back one of the men.

As they rowed closer to take the supplies we offered, two of them desperately tried to board our boat. We insisted that this was impossible, that it was illegal for us to bring them to the US. Our captain, Craig Jiovani, radioed the location of their boat to the Coast Guard. A dispatcher told him to wait with the Cubans until help arrived. We tossed the refugees the supplies and talked.

The men were from the Havana suburb of La Lisa Marianao. They told us they paid $2,000 for their scraggly boat — the *Mariel* — and the rusted old five-horsepower engine which had broken down on their second day at sea. The money came from relatives living in Florida. One said he had been a civilian plumber for the army; another had worked in a store in Havana. Although they looked young and healthy, a few of them were badly sunburned and seemed dazed and lost as their boat took water.

We warned them that the Coast Guard would take them to Guantanamo Naval Base, not to the US. "They could take us to Alaska, we don't care," replied Pedro Zamon Rodriguez, "just as long as we get out of Cuba."

As we waited for the *Gallatin*, the Coast Guard cutter that this week alone has pulled thousands of Cubans from these waters, two charter boats packed with television crews who had heard our radio transmission pulled up to snare footage for the five o'clock news. Like sea vultures, these reporters swooped in and, without so much as offering a jug of water to the castaways, took pictures and left. The Cubans were becoming agitated. We'd been with them an hour and a half and still no Coast Guard. A rain squall hit and the men grew more desperate. We yelled at them not to worry, that we'd wait until rescuers arrived.

Finally, the Coast Guard steamed toward us. We watched from a few hundred yards away as the rowboat was pulled alongside the cutter and the men were taken on board. As they climbed up the gangway, each of them turned to wave at us. Now that they were safe, we headed back to Key West. "My family lost its boat in the Mariel boatlift," said the *Grand Slam*'s mate, Spencer. "Me and my father leased our boat to some Cubans and we went down to Miami to pick up their family," he recalled. "We waited there a week. When we left with twenty-eight people, one of those big concrete ferries in the harbor backed into us and tore a hole in the boat. We sank five miles out to sea. Another boat picked us up."

That was in 1980. Fourteen years later, his father long since buried, Spencer was again saving Cuban refugees. In Key West, I realized, that seems to go with the territory.

When we returned to dry land, I tried to contact the Florida-based relatives of the *Mariel* crew with the telephone numbers they had shouted out to me. Twenty-four hours later, I had spoken with most of the families and even visited Mireya Suarez, a cleaning woman whose son Israel and son-in-law Pedro were now en route to Guantanamo. Mireya left Cuba three years ago; she visited the US as a tourist and never returned. "My son's been trying to get out since 1980 and so has my husband," she told me in the living room of her sparsely furnished house in Little Havana. "Our whole family is against Fidel."

A few blocks away on Calle Ocho, Cuban-Americans were increasingly divided over recent White House policy toward this new wave of immigrants. For her part, Suarez is amazed that some Cuban-Americans are urging those still on the island not to leave. She is astounded that leaders such as Jorge Mas Canosa, the head of the powerful Cuban-American National Foundation, have endorsed President Clinton's policy of shipping the boat people to the US military base in Guantanamo. Mas Canosa, a hard-core conservative Republican who couldn't even get a phone call returned from the White House a year ago, was happy as a clam last Friday to be granted a meeting with Clinton. During that session, rumor has it, Mas Canosa cut a deal with the president: in return for tougher sanctions against Cuba, such as the suspension of air travel and money transfers, his group would back the Guantanamo detention policy. Suarez's opinion? "Either he's an imbecile or a Communist, and I'll tell him to his face."

The last thing Mas Canosa would expect to be called is a Communist, but in this fractious exile community this is the ultimate putdown, worse than being called a mass murderer. As Suarez sees it, "These Cubans who came here years ago have their nice houses and good jobs and no family left over there. And now they tell the rest of us to stay. Why didn't they say that back in 1959?"

In the case of Mas Canosa, the reason is not hard to discern. This shrewd politico, who does not hide his ambition to be next president of Cuba, wants dissatisfied Cubans to remain on the island to bring the economically troubled country to the brink of revolution. His stance, however, has angered many people. Pedro Gonzalez, for instance, spent twenty-one years as a political prisoner in Cuba. Now he lies on a cot on Calle Ocho in the shadow of a memorial to Cubans who died in the failed CIA-sponsored Bay of Pigs invasion more than thirty years ago. Gonzalez is on the seventh day of a hunger strike. When asked about Mas Canosa, he replied, "Some of our leaders are putting their personal interests above those of the people."

One of the many anti-Castro Cubans who view the refugee city the US Navy is creating in Guantanamo as a potential base from which to attack the Castro regime, Gonzalez is looking to the future for strength: "We don't want any help from the US. We'll do our own fighting." Meanwhile, in Cuba, another wily politician has declared that anyone who wants to leave is free to go. So, in this strange new world order of ours, we have Castro offering freedom to the refugees and Clinton promising to lock them up if they take the offer . . .

ALL WEEKEND THE men had been waiting for the seas to calm. They had dragged their makeshift raft across the fine sandy beach and built a small hut nearby in which to sleep at night. "If the weather breaks, we leave tomorrow at four A.M.," Rogelio Arame explained, "and hundreds of others are planning to leave too."

Arame told me this at noon on the Santa Maria public beach, 20 miles east of Havana. The day was broiling hot. On one end of the beach, three rafts were clearly visible with about a score of people camped beside them; at the other end, hundreds of Cuban families and young lovers, enjoying a summer day at the shore, just ignored the dissidents. Arame's crew of young electricians, plumbers and cooks posed eagerly in front of their vessel. Crude but solid, it was made of large planks surrounded with inner tubes and Styrofoam, a metal rudder, notches for six oars and a rounded bow fashioned from fiberglass.

Israel Roque Borrero, a compass hanging from a chain on his bare chest, showed a visitor his passport and a letter from the US

Immigration and Naturalization Service. It was dated June 15, and it informed him that his request for a visa for political asylum had been denied. Roque Borrero, a plumber, said he had tried to escape once before and had been sent to jail for three months. "I don't understand why they wouldn't give me a visa," he said. "I've been a political prisoner, isn't that enough?"

Carlos Puig, a lanky, long-haired bookseller and poet who said he'd decided to put out to sea with his friends "for the experience," acted as the group's bilingual spokesman. "Notice that we are all workers, not like the criminals that left from Mariel fourteen years ago.

"We are not confused," he added. "We know the US government would rather Cubans flee in boats than give us visas. Fidel looks worse that way, even if some of us drown. We are caught between the posturing of both governments."

The poet is right. The sad truth of this tragic raft exodus is that if for the past five or six years our own government had been processing the 20,000 allowable immigrant visas instead of the 3,000 or so the stingy INS grants annually, you would have had 100,000 more Cubans living legally in the US instead of this uncertain ocean anarchy.

A few miles closer to Havana, on the rocky beach of the fishing town of Cojimar, hundreds of people stood watching while other rafters made last minute preparations. Many of the townspeople debated whether the rafters were brave or ignorant. "If they could do it normally, maybe half the country would leave," said one man named Alejandro. "But this way, it's crazy."

Over on Havana's famous Malecon boulevard, where thousands of Cubans lounge along the sea wall on weekends and evenings, a steady stream of young prostitutes try to pick up foreign tourists. This weekend the national debate over the raft exodus could be heard wherever young people gathered. Saturday evening, for instance, Pedro and Luis – they wouldn't give their last names – were carting their raft, a few planks of wood and Styrofoam tied together, on a bicycle along the Malecon. Their feet and the raft were covered with black grease balls. "We left this morning, but the water was too rough," Luis said. "And that bay is too dirty. After three hours we came back. We'll try again Monday morning." A few blocks away, young hustlers trying to sell cigars laughed at the refugees. "Those who leave are the weak ones," said a man named Luigi. "In this country you can make a living on the black market. But you have to know how. Do you want good cigars, real cheap?"

A few weeks ago a riot broke out among young people fed up with the Castro regime. When it was reported that the protesters were breaking store windows and fighting with police near the Malecon, Castro went to the scene himself, bolted from his black Mercedes, and, against the wishes of his bodyguards, walked the streets to assess the situation. "I saw him that day," said one young Cuban woman. "He was so angry at these people so he told them, 'If you don't like Cuba, then leave.'"

Unless leaders from Havana and Washington hammer out some kind of agreement soon, Castro seems perfectly willing to let even half the country take to the sea. The time to end the posturing, human decency tells you, is now . . .

His NAME IS Dale. He is an American businessman making fistfuls of dollars in a country our own nation has boycotted for thirty-two years. Her name is Dianys. She is a 23-year-old pharmaceutical chemist, but in her spare time she struts Havana's numerous broad avenues, like the oceanside Malecon, and lounges in the lobbies of the city's bustling downtown hotels.

For obvious reasons, both Dale and Dianys prefer that their last names not be used. US capitalist dollars and rampant prostitution were once the twin evils of the old Cuba: the Cuba of the dictator Fulgencio Batista, of Meyer Lansky and the mob, of United Fruit Co., and the First National City Bank. Dollars and prostitution became the odious symbols of Cuba's corruption. In 1959, Fidel Castro came along and swore to sweep the evils away with his Socialist revolution.

Today, thousands of Cubans, desperate and weary from three decades of life after that revolution and from Washington's equally long embargo, are fleeing the island for Florida. Some come for freedom, others for VCRs. Yet even as the rafts set sail, the two old enemies of the revolution continue their startling comeback. "There's more American businessmen in Cuba than anyone realizes," said Dale. "Everyone's waiting for the US embargo to end. We know it's not a question of if, but when."

Meanwhile, Bill Clinton readies his assistants to meet with Castro's people in New York, supposedly to discuss controlling immigration. This is all Clinton is prepared to discuss with Castro – and his reluctance to speak further with the Cuban leader is foolish and hypocritical. We trade with China, which is just as Communist as Cuba, only bigger and richer. We trade with Vietnam, which killed 55,000 of our young men in a war. We're even talking to North Korea. Not to talk to or trade with Cuba, which is only 90 miles from our shores and does business with everyone except us, is lunacy.

Dale works for a British outfit and knows well the consequences of US trade policy. "The British and French companies are the ones who don't want the embargo to end," he said. "Right now, they have no competition from the US." Dale buys and sells yachts out of Marina Hemingway and much of his business is with Americans. "We had a regatta of ninety boats that came down from Sarasota in June," he said. "You think the American kids in those boats didn't spend dollars in the country?" Dale even told me of Texas boaters who regularly bring Americans to Cuba to fish in the country's lakes. "The biggest bass in the world are supposed to be in those lakes," he said.

As for Dianys, her pursuit of US dollars is less enthusiastic. Last Saturday night, I found her and her two girlfriends, all stuffed into skintight minidresses, loitering in the Hotel Riviera's ornate lobby bar. They were trying to land a few foreign tourists for the night. At one table sat a well-heeled geezer from Spain with a gorgeous young woman on each arm. The beauties looked young enough to be his granddaughters. Later that night, I saw him slip some bills to a hotel security guard and take the girls up to his room.

Some of the local women who work the Riviera are tired of depending on a food rationing system which leaves them little to eat. For most of them, the goal of their flirting is only a nutritious free meal in the hotel's restaurant. Others are just trying to get someone to pay the $10 admission to the hotel's enormous nightclub, which is jammed each weekend with 2,000 gyrating Cubans and tourists. Most, though, are willing to do anything for American dollars. Havana's nightlife has become so wild that regular charter flights arrive each weekend from the Bahamas, Jamaica and Mexico, carrying scores of young men out for a good time.

Dianys's monthly salary from her pharmacy job will only buy a few US dollars. These days, the gap between dollars and pesos has grown so large that the only people who can survive adequately in Cuba are workers in the giant tourist industry – or those like Dianys who live off it. "Going with tourists is my only hope right now," she said. "I don't have any family in America, so I don't want to go to Miami. I just want what normal people have in other countries."

As for the US embargo, it is mostly a matter of currency. If you have dollars, you can buy whatever you want. "I go to the store and ask for Gatorade," said businessman Dale, "and they answer, 'What flavor?' If the first store doesn't stock Dove soap, the next one does."

When Clinton and Castro meet in New York this week, both will be well aware that those old evils – dollars and prostitution – are back with a vengeance. Everything else is so much hot air . . .

FIDEL CASTRO'S SOCIALIST government is about to make one more concession to capitalism by allowing Cuban farmers to sell their produce on the open market. After three years of economic crises – which have made for scarcities of food and gasoline and fueled recent upsurges in the numbers of raft people – Castro and his top aides have chosen to imitate prosperous China's model of mixing Socialist politics with capitalist economics. The new agricultural policy is expected to be announced officially in the next few weeks.

Under the plan, private farmers who still control about 10 percent of Cuba's arable land will now compete with state-owned farms and agricultural cooperatives. In addition, Cubans who tend garden vegetable plots will also be allowed to sell their produce and pocket the profits. "There is no contradiction between a Socialist system and a peasant free market," said Carlos Lage, the architect of many of the country's recent economic reforms. During a long interview Friday night, Lage, the balding and charismatic first secretary of Cuba's State Council — and the man often mentioned as a possible successor to Castro — insisted that Cuba had experimented with open peasant markets in the early 1980s and that they had proven successful.

The new agricultural policy follows a string of other recent reforms that have moved Cuba closer to Western-style capitalism than ever before. Among those changes:

- Opening more than 100 joint business ventures with foreign companies, mostly European, Canadian and Mexican.
- Expanding the country's tourist industry: for the first time Cuba will earn more money this year from tourism than from sugar exports.
- Allowing Cubans to hold dollars, an acknowledgment that US currency has become critical to the country's economy.
- Allowing Cubans to become vendors or run small businesses, a move that has resulted in the establishment of more than 160,000 self-employed enterprises since the beginning of the year.
- Cutting government subsidies to unprofitable enterprises.
- Beginning a system of taxation in a country that has never had one and increasing prices for electricity, water, school lunches and other basic necessities.
- Leasing 6.2 million acres of state-owned lands to farm cooperatives for cultivation.
- Ending the system of unlimited-length unemployment insurance at 60 percent of previous pay for workers.

Lage insisted that the reforms did not mean an end to the 35-year-old Socialist revolution. But what does one make of a revolution where prostitution flourishes, where the US dollar is king, and where the majority can barely find enough to eat while foreigners and a handful of Cubans are now free to amass wealth? When asked whether he thought Cubans would not soon resent all the foreign tourists in Cuba, Lage admitted that the reforms had already created "some inequality" which Castro's revolution had once vowed to end. But he argued that these changes in policy were necessary to stabilize the economy, given the recent loss of aid from the former Soviet Union and the tightening of the thirty-year US embargo. When asked if the changes weren't really an acknowledgment that socialism as a system had failed, Lage said he rejected that view. He predicted that certain gains of the revolution, in education, health care and worker protection, would never be sacrificed. "In an orderly fashion, a Socialist system can do anything," he said.

Cuba's leaders have carefully watched the social chaos that accompanied the collapse of the Soviet Union, Yugoslavia and other European Socialist countries. They are determined to follow the examples set by China and Vietnam, instead of Russia and Yugoslavia, and to mix capitalist reform with authoritarian governmental control. As our government plans its next steps toward Cuba, it would do well to ask if it wishes to push Cuba into becoming another Russia or another China . . .

THREE RAFTS CRAMMED with people had already hit the water by late yesterday morning. They drifted slowly offshore, without motors, even without oars, as they tried to catch the elusive Gulf Stream that could carry them ninety miles to Florida. Back on the beach at Cojimar, knots of bare-chested men worked feverishly to finish a half-dozen other rafts. Time, after all, was running out.

Everyone here knew that in New York City, Cuban and US officials had just reached an accord to stop the incredible migration of

Cubans from these shores. For weeks that tragic exodus has shocked America. It has focused attention on Cuba and our 3-decade-long blockade to a degree unheard of since Nikita Khrushchev and Jack Kennedy almost blew up the world over some missiles. At long last, the White House sat down and reasoned with Fidel Castro's government, just as we have with every other Communist government on the planet. And reason had led to some understanding. Not acceptance. Not friendship. Just understanding.

The agreement calls for at least 20,000 Cubans to be allowed into the US each year from those already on waiting lists in Cuba, regardless of whether they have immediate family in the US or not. In addition, an undetermined number with family members who are US citizens will also be admitted. The accord, however, also continues the new White House policy of not granting automatic entry to Cuban raft people and of sending those who are intercepted at sea to Guantanamo Bay or Panama. It also commits our government to punish those who hijack planes or boats from Cuba to the US. In return, Castro has agreed to prevent Cubans from fleeing his country. In official broadcasts and in newspapers yesterday, Cubans were warned that after noon on Tuesday, all those fleeing will be stopped and any rafts found on the island's beaches will be confiscated.

In Cojimar, Castro's warnings had not fallen on deaf ears. "I don't know how, but I'll be out of here by then," said 20-year-old Thomas Rivera. Rivera was staring at a sturdy but empty 12-foot boat moored, complete with its rusty engine, among the rocks. "The owner wants $3,000 for this thing," Rivera said. "If enough of us get together, we can buy it." As I stood on the beach with Rivera and his friends, two interior ministry soldiers arrived and announced to the crowd that starting Tuesday they would "use force if necessary" to stop anyone from leaving.

Margarita Machin's only son fled on a raft a week ago. "I don't know what's happened to him, but at least he's out of this country," she said. "Now it's my turn." A few yards away from her, gray-haired, wiry Emilio Carranza stood guard over a raft that had two long, empty water tanks attached as flotation devices. The tanks had been fitted with metal cones at one end that made them look like rockets. "I'm just watching this for a relative who's leaving tonight," he explained. "I'll never leave my country. I just want a better life than I have now."

August 24–September 13, 1994

POSTSCRIPT:
NEW YORK, 1995

IT WAS SUPPOSED to be just another police shooting in this new era of law and order. The official account in the newspapers the next day seemed fairly open and shut: two Hispanic men forced their way into a South Bronx tenement apartment on the night of January 11, 1995, robbed a young couple, then threatened to return the next night. But when the men knocked on the door of the apartment with a third man the following night, two police detectives responding to the couple's frightened call were waiting inside. The detectives burst from the kitchen and ordered the intruders, each of whom had a gun hidden on him, to put their hands in the air and drop to the floor. The men resisted. A shoot-out erupted. When the smoke cleared, two of the robbers were dead. Multiple gunshot wounds to the front, side and back, reported the city medical examiner. As if to put the final exclamation point to this official story, a police spokesman told the press all three men had criminal records.

Case closed.

Well, not quite. Something didn't make sense as I read the account. Why would robbers warn their victims they were coming back? I decided to look a little closer, especially since one of the detectives in the case had been involved a few years earlier in the vicious, off-duty beating of a fellow black detective.

The official story, I soon discovered, was riddled with more holes than the two dead men. During the next few months I kept peeling away at the layers of confusion and deceit that enveloped the incident. First, police clarified that none of the "robbers" had fired their guns, while the two detectives had unleashed a fusillade of twenty-six shots, hitting the dead men twenty-two times. The "shoot-out" suddenly became a "shoot-in."

The surviving intruder, an 18-year-old named Fred Bonilla,

claimed that he and his friends had already surrendered and were on the ground when police opened fire. Still, I was not about to believe the word of a teenager caught in a robbery against two hero detectives. But then the families of the dead men secured their own pathologist, who concluded that the city medical examiner's report was wrong: all the bullets – fourteen in one man and eight in the other – had pierced their bodies from the rear or side, none from the front. After I reported that new revelation, the city medical examiner hastily changed his conclusion. A doctor had misread a wound chart, the examiner's office admitted.

I followed with a report that the alleged robbery had not even been a robbery! In fact, the couple in the apartment were running an illegal marriage ring, where they paid citizens to marry undocumented immigrants so they could be naturalized. The young men who came to the door, two of whom had only a previous juvenile conviction for disorderly conduct, were friends of a young disgruntled woman to whom the couple in the apartment owed money from one of those illegal marriages. The men had come to collect the money owed to the young woman.

Before long, I started getting phone calls and letters from anonymous detectives. The tipsters insisted the shooting was being covered up because the two detectives were former bodyguards of Mayor Rudy Giuliani, and one was a boyhood friend of the mayor's.

In the midst of these revelations, and after a Bronx grand jury voted to absolve the officers of wrongdoing, one of the jurors contacted me. The vote in the secret proceeding had been very close, the juror said, even though the prosecutor had steered the jury toward no indictment. I decided to keep digging for facts. In a subsequent column I reported that investigators for the city's Civilian Complaint Review Board (CCRB), the agency charged with probing police abuse complaints, concluded that both dead men were shot numerous times while lying on the floor on their stomachs. Another column revealed that police from the local precinct improperly helped move the couple who lived in the apartment to new housing, hid the couple's whereabouts from the CCRB investigators, and tried to prevent investigators from subpoenaing the pair to give testimony. I reported further that the mayor's office had shown uncommon interest in the case. In late July, the CCRB concluded that the two dead men had not drawn guns against the police. Instead, the agency ruled that detectives had used "unnecessary force" in arresting them. By this time, the public uproar in the Hispanic community over the case had prompted the US Justice Department to begin a probe of possible civil rights violations.

Instead of carefully reviewing the results of the review board's investigation, the city's police commissioner immediately blasted the agency as unprofessional. The mayor's own Department of Investigations suddenly opened a wide-ranging probe of the agency's work. Police sources began leaking information to friendly reporters to make the agency appear out of control.

Thus, the watchdog agency legally charged with monitoring police abuse itself became the target of investigation. As of this writing, the federal probe into the police shooting of Anthony Rosario and Hilton Vega is not concluded. But the case has already revealed in chilling fashion how far some guardians of law and order will go to obstruct a search for the truth.

The case confirms my belief that the criminal justice industry, both in its public and private forms, is the fastest growing, least monitored and potentially most dangerous force in American society today. Mushrooming construction of prisons. Increased production of high-tech surveillance and control systems for the public. Skyrocketing budgets for law enforcement and court personnel while other parts of government spending shrink. Tougher sentencing laws creating record prison populations. The steady erosion of individual rights and the presumption of innocence by the courts and legislators. All of these trends are inching our nation closer to a police state. The streets of Santo Domingo, after all, were never safer than under Trujillo, Moscow's never freer of violent crime than under Stalin, and Berlin's never more orderly than under Hitler. Meanwhile, we in the mass media, by nurturing the public frenzy with one lurid tale of violent crime after another, by failing too often to investigate diligently and report the most horrific examples of police and government abuse of citizens' rights, are unwittingly preparing the soil for such a police state, one where blacks, Hispanics and immigrants will undoubtedly become the main target of its wrath.

With minorities and immigrants now a majority in most of the nation's big cities, it is no surprise that the rise of law-and-order politicians parallels the coming to power, in both the Democratic and Republican parties, of anti-urban interests based in suburbia. In this, the media are no exception. The dominance of television news, where the stark image is always preferred to nuanced analysis, over big-city newspapers signals the eclipsing of the complex information needs of a diverse urban population in favor of the homogenized needs of suburbia. Television stations, after all, reach further and deeper into the population than do newspapers. They broadcast beyond the urban center to the wealthier suburban fringes, spreading images of crime and chaos from the city core far beyond its borders. Gradually, in the consciousness of the manicured lawns and picture-perfect living rooms of suburbia, the vision takes root of an inner-city hell, of urban areas teeming with all that is evil and wasteful in American life.

Any balanced appreciation that our cities remain the nexus of wealth, social vibrancy and cohesion for America's regions becomes lost. The cities, lest we forget, provide police protection not just to their own residents but to the legions of suburbanites who stream in each day on urban public transportation systems and highways, to office buildings, theaters, restaurants, medical centers and universities, institutions which provide jobs and modern amenities for everyone in the region, not just the city residents. At night, the suburbanites retire to sleepy townships and rural communities which boast none of these things.

The city of Trenton, for instance, has long been considered one of New Jersey's urban eyesores. Located in the middle of the state, it was once a blue-collar manufacturing center and, for years, as visitors entered town they could see a large sign spanning one of its bridges: "Trenton Makes: The World Takes." Today in America, it is the suburbs which constantly milk the wealth that our cities provide them – the best jobs, the transportation, the culture.

Meanwhile, back in the inner city, blacks and Hispanics, who are now the majority in virtually all the great metropolises of America, are relatively powerless to stop the nation's disinvestment in its urban infrastructure. Whether it be roads, bridges, parks, hospitals, public schools, libraries or community centers, our inner cities are decaying at a frightening rate. Government refuses basic maintenance precisely because the cities are now so black and brown that the wealthy downtown enclaves and well-to-do suburban areas simply will not allow it.

Nearly half of all New York City's 37,000 police officers, for example, live in the suburbs. If the city wanted to reduce its unemployment and increase its tax base, it could simply require all future cops to be city residents. But suburban politicians in the state capital have repeatedly thwarted efforts by several mayors to change residency laws for cops. Even the move to privatize government has become a means to cannibalize many urban city services and contract them out to low-wage companies where, in the name of efficiency, government-subsidized profits go to suburban entrepreneurs. Anti-urban interests know the political deck is stacked in their favor, especially at the national level, where under our federal system rural states with small populations, such as South Dakota, Idaho and Utah, have as many votes in the US Senate as giant, highly urbanized states like New York, California and Illinois.

In the 1980s, though, a new political direction emerged in urban politics that frightened the established order: the country's two largest minority groups, and the heart of the big-city electorate, African Americans and Hispanics, began to unite as a voting block. The mayoral victories of Harold Washington in Chicago, Wilson Goode in Philadelphia and David Dinkins in New York City – each bringing to power the first black mayor in the history of those cities – were the signposts of that new direction. The previous decade had seen scores of black mayors elected in majority black cities, but this time black candidates won their elections by building a strong alliance with the growing Hispanic community. In each case, the black mayoral candidate won more than 60 percent of the Hispanic vote. Faced with racially polarized contests, Hispanics chose to ally with the black and more liberal candidate. The Washington and Goode victories in 1983 prompted Jesse Jackson to run for president under the banner of a new Rainbow Coalition. Jackson's surprise showings in both 1984 and 1988, especially his success in registering millions of new voters, further unnerved the nation's political elite.

But the Rainbow Coalition proved more dream than reality, one where Hispanic, Asian and white progressive activists often felt shunted aside into an unequal partnership by veteran black politicians, many of whom had risen to power through the old and corrupted Democratic party big-city machines. After Harold Washington died, many Hispanic leaders in Chicago threw their support to a white Democrat, Richard Daley Jr, while in Philadelphia, several Hispanic leaders did likewise, switching to Democrat Ed Rendell after Goode concluded his maximum of two terms in office.

Finally, in 1993, the black–Latino coalition in New York City foundered during the re-election campaign of David Dinkins. While Dinkins retained a majority of Latino votes, both his percentage and the turnout in the Latino community dropped, enabling Republican Rudy Giuliani to squeak to victory with a very slim margin. Thus, by 1995, the mayoralty in four of the country's largest cities – New York, Los Angeles, Chicago and Philadelphia – had reverted from a liberal or moderate black incumbent to a more conservative white leader. In each case, Hispanic voters shifted in significant percentages from a previous black candidate to the new white candidate, and each time the argument of those who switched sounded the same: "We weren't treated as equals by the black leaders." Meanwhile, the failure of Jesse Jackson to expand his Rainbow Coalition through a third presidential campaign in 1992 left the movement organizationally adrift at the national level. Even as the number of black and Hispanic leaders in Congress reached a record number, the cohesiveness of the alliance fractured on several issues, especially as a large percentage of black voters, along with much of white America, became increasingly uneasy with the explosion of the country's Hispanic and Asian population. In November of 1994, for instance, a majority of black Californians voted for Proposition 187 to cut off all public benefits to illegal immigrants.

Thus, the Rainbow Coalition as an organizational vehicle to weld a new progressive alliance was on its deathbed by early 1995. Instead, Hispanics, along with the growing Asian American population, began to come of age as a new and unpredictable "Third Force" in the ethnic cauldron of American political life. Both groups overwhelmingly reject today's fashionable conservative view that racial and ethnic inequality are things of the past. But Hispanics and Asians also increasingly reject the racial fixation in national politics of black vs. white, for they are neither. Hispanics, themselves an amalgam of races, seek a more equitable multiracial coalition, one that cares about the future of the cities in which they find themselves overwhelmingly concentrated. Such a new majority, fashioned largely from disenfranchised and forgotten working-class Americans who do not normally vote, may also refuse to accept the worn partisan divisions of Democrat vs. Republican.

Urban America is fed up with those conservative demagogues who seized the national spotlight the past twenty years in the name of law and order and diverted public attention to racial squabbling between everyday Americans, while their corporate friends fled abroad in search of cheap labor, prodded government to ignore the decay of the cities, gutted trade unions, eroded the living standards of American workers, and amassed unparalleled wealth.

In the neighborhoods of forgotten urban America, rage gathers in the shadows. Quadruple the jail cells and you will not lock it up. Break all the unions and you will not chase it away. Urban America wants decent jobs, not part-time work at lower hourly wages than ten years ago. Its people want to know that a single illness will not drive them into poverty. They want clean parks and the kinds of schools that give their children a chance at success, just like those kids from the suburbs. They are tired of suburban white America regarding the black and brown cities with dread instead of hope, as enemies instead of partners, as alien instead of family.

We either heed the rage or wait for it to spring from the shadows.

Juan Gonzalez
August, 1995